The Avon International
COOKBOOK

Winning Recipes from Avon Representatives Around the World

This seal assures you that every recipe in
The Avon International Cook Book is tested
and approved by the Better Homes and
Gardens® Test Kitchen. Each recipe is
tested for family appeal, practicality, and
deliciousness.

Produced by Meredith Publishing Services, Locust at 17th, Des Moines, IA 50336.
©Meredith Corporation, 1983. All Rights Reserved. Printed in the U.S.A.

Welcome

to the wide and friendly world of Avon. In this unique cook book, Avon Representatives from 29 countries share their favorite recipes--the foods these busy women like to cook for their families and friends. You'll find delicious main dishes and salads, hearty soups, wholesome vegetables and breads, and luscious desserts. You can treat your family to a taste of Latin America, or serve guests a traditional dish from the South Pacific, or make a classic casserole from western Europe for a potluck supper.

Every recipe in this collection has been tested by the Better Homes and Gardens® Test Kitchen and adapted to use familiar ingredients, measurements, and methods.

Avon Representatives around the world hope you'll enjoy their recipes and wish you and your family "Bon Appétit."

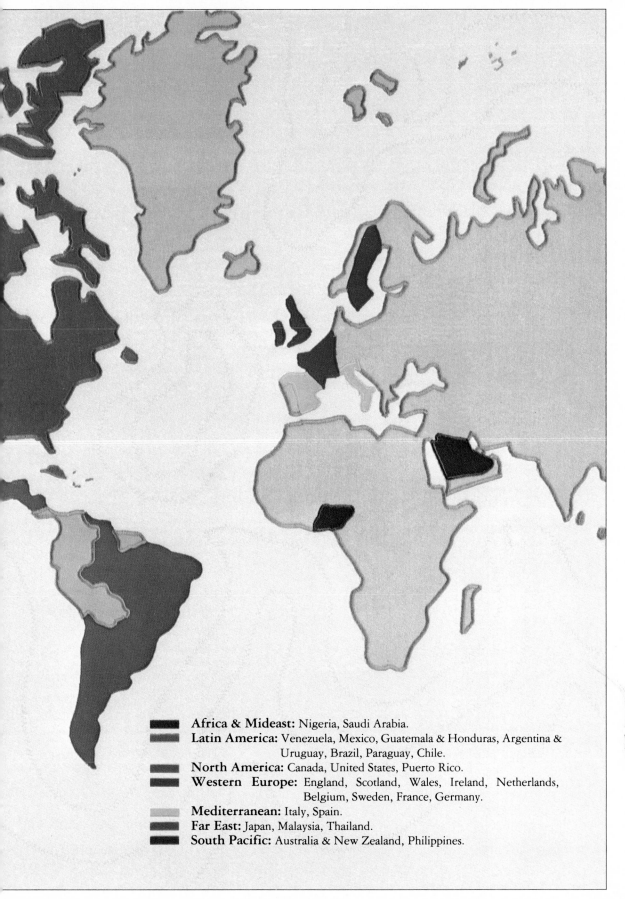

Africa & Mideast: Nigeria, Saudi Arabia.
Latin America: Venezuela, Mexico, Guatemala & Honduras, Argentina & Uruguay, Brazil, Paraguay, Chile.
North America: Canada, United States, Puerto Rico.
Western Europe: England, Scotland, Wales, Ireland, Netherlands, Belgium, Sweden, France, Germany.
Mediterranean: Italy, Spain.
Far East: Japan, Malaysia, Thailand.
South Pacific: Australia & New Zealand, Philippines.

AFRICA & MIDEAST

Nigeria   6-11
Groundnut Stew (main dish)
Jollof Rice (main dish)

Saudi Arabia
Green Beans and Shrimp (vegetable)
Pita Bread (bread)
Macaroni with Tomato-Almond Sauce (side dish)
Figs in Syrup (dessert)

LATIN AMERICA

Venezuela   12-25
Beef Stew (soup)
Baked Snapper Fillets (main dish)
Three-Way Cheese Ball (appetizer)

Mexico
Rolled Shrimp Canapés (appetizer)
Crackling Salad (salad)
Fish Veracruz (main dish)
Mexican Chocolate Cake (dessert)

Guatemala & Honduras
Spicy Meatball Soup (soup)
Bread and Wine Dessert (dessert)

Argentina & Uruguay
Apple Dessert (dessert)
Bacon-Pepperoni Bread (bread)
Fruit Salad (salad)

Brazil
Brigadeiros (candy)
Honey-Spice Bread (bread)

Paraguay
Cheese Pie (main dish)
Layered Corn Pie (main dish)

Chile
Beans Granados (vegetable)
Empanadas (main dish)

NORTH AMERIC

Canada   26-53
Appetizer Lobster Rolls (appetizer)
Drop Sugar Cookies (dessert)
Rhubarb Upside-Down Cake (dessert)
Stove-Top Meatballs (main dish)
Tourtière (main dish)

United States
French Quarter Bean Soup (soup)
California Cheese Soup (soup)
Mini Cheese Tarts (appetizer)
Marinated Mushrooms and Olives (appetizer)
Three-Wheat Batter Bread (bread)
Beer Biscuits (bread)
Molded Buttermilk Salad (bread)
Broccoli-Cauliflower Salad (salad)
Garden Potato Salad (salad)
Herbed Zucchini (vegetable)
Wild Rice Supreme (side dish)
Cheese-Scalloped Carrots (vegetable)
Hash Brown Potato Casserole (vegetable)
Fish Florentine (main dish)
Hunter-Style Chicken (main dish)
Southwestern Pocket Sandwiches (main dish)
Broccoli-Rice Casserole (side dish)
Pasta Pizza Squares (main dish)
Sausage and Potato Bake (main dish)
Beef Roast and Noodles (main dish)
Peachy Meat Loaf Pie (main dish)
Oven-Style Pork Ribs (main dish)
Red Raspberry Cream Cheese Pie (dessert)
Freezer Peanut Butter Pie (dessert)
Peanut Butter Chocolate Chip Cookies (dessert)
Best Chocolate Brownies (desert)
Apple Harvest Cake (dessert)
Sour Cream Pecan Pound Cake (dessert)
Banana Split Dessert (dessert)

Puerto Rico
Rice-Garbanzo Bake (main dish)
Fried Chicken (main dish)
Sweet Potato-Pumpkin Puddings (dessert)

WESTERN EUROPE

54-73

England
Yorkshire Curd Tart (dessert)
Rabbit-Cider Casserole (main dish)

Scotland
Treacle Tea Scones (bread)
Cock-a-Leekie Soup (soup)

Wales
Lamb with Honey (main dish)
Onion Cake (vegetable)
Bara Brith (bread)

Ireland
Gaelic Chops (main dish)
Colcannon (vegetable)

Netherlands
Gelderland Stew (soup)
Fruited Buttermilk Ring (dessert)

Belgium
Ostend Waterzooi (soup)
Glazed Onions (vegetable)
Stuffed Bacon Rolls (main dish)

Sweden
Ham Roll-Ups (main dish)
Lingonberry Ice Cream (dessert)
Herring in Cream Sauce (appetizer)

France
Strawberries and Cream Cake (dessert)
Cheese Puff (bread)
Veal Birds (main dish)
Nut Torte (dessert)
Crab Soufflé (main dish)
Potato Pie (vegetable)
Crème Fraîche (dessert sauce)

Germany
Bavarian Doughnut Puffs (bread)
Fish and Clam Chowder (soup)
Smoked Pork Chops with Sauerkraut (main dish)
Meatballs with Buttermilk Gravy (main dish)
Sauerbraten (main dish)
Spaetzle (side dish)

MEDITERRANEAN

74-79

Italy
Eggplant Parmigiana (vegetable)
Minestrone (soup)
Antipasto Volante (appetizer)

Spain
Cod and Potato Bake (main dish)
Chocolate Cream (dessert)

FAR EAST

80-89

Japan
Broiled Ginger Pork (main dish)
Sukiyaki (main dish)
Teppenyaki (main dish)
Yakimono (main dish)
Green Beans with Miso Dressing (vegetable)
Fried Chicken Wings (appetizer)

Malaysia
Fried Beef Bundles (main dish)
Pineapple Pastries (dessert)
Malaysian Stir-Fried Chicken (main dish)

Thailand
Panang Meatballs (main dish)
Thai Shrimp Salad (main dish)

SOUTH PACIFIC

90-95

Australia & New Zealand
Kiwi Cream Pie (dessert)
Pavlova (dessert)
Spicy Meat Loaf (main dish)

Philippines
Lumpia (main dish)
Coconut Macaroon Cupcakes (dessert)

AFRICA &

MIDEAST

Nigeria

In a whirlwind of change and progress in Nigeria, food customs are changing, too. Fish is becoming more popular, an important switch for a country where chicken has long been the main protein food. Meals are usually based on a stew or soup accompanied by a starchy food, such as rice, yams, plantains, and bananas. One of the most popular chicken-rice recipes is Jollof Rice, which has become the traditional Sunday dinner dish in many homes and restaurants. Sauces are often thickened with bean or yam puree and spiced with red peppers. Coconut is a staple in every kitchen. It's not just for dessert or candy, but is an ingredient in sauces and is served fresh as an accompaniment to the main course. Even the coconut milk is used in cooking.

GROUNDNUT STEW

English colonists called peanuts groundnuts, giving this celebrated West African dish its unusual name--

 1 2½- to 3-pound broiler-fryer
    chicken, cut up
 3 tablespoons cooking oil
 1 pound beef stew meat, cut
    into 1-inch pieces
 2 medium onions, chopped
 1 medium green pepper,
    chopped
 1 28-ounce can tomatoes,
    cut up
 1 teaspoon salt
 1 to 2 teaspoons ground
    red pepper
 ¾ cup peanut butter
    Mashed sweet potatoes or
    hot cooked rice

In a large saucepan or Dutch oven brown chicken pieces in hot oil about 15 minutes; remove from pan. Set aside, reserving drippings. Add beef, onion, and green pepper to drippings; cook till beef is brown and onion is tender. Drain off fat. Stir in *undrained* tomatoes, salt, and red pepper. Bring to boiling; reduce heat. Cover; simmer 30 minutes. Add chicken pieces; simmer 20 minutes more. In small saucepan melt peanut butter over low heat. Stir into chicken mixture. Return mixture to boiling; reduce heat. Cover; simmer 20 minutes more. Skim off fat. Serve with mashed sweet potatoes or hot cooked rice. Makes 8 to 10 servings.

JOLLOF RICE

 1 2½- to 3-pound broiler-fryer
    chicken, cut up
 2 tablespoons peanut oil or
    cooking oil
 1 medium onion, chopped
 1 16-ounce can tomatoes,
    cut up
 1¼ cups chicken broth
 1 bay leaf
 ½ teaspoon ground ginger,
    ground cinnamon, or dried
    thyme, crushed
 ½ teaspoon salt
 ¼ teaspoon ground red pepper
 1 cup long grain rice
 1 tablespoon snipped parsley

In a large skillet brown chicken pieces on both sides in hot oil about 15 minutes; remove from skillet. Set chicken aside, reserving drippings. Add the onion to drippings; cook till tender but not brown. Drain off fat. Return chicken to skillet. Combine *undrained* tomatoes; chicken broth; bay leaf; ginger, cinnamon, or thyme; salt; and ground red pepper. Pour over chicken. *Do not stir.* Bring to boiling; reduce heat. Cover; simmer for 30 minutes. Skim off fat. Add the rice, making sure all the rice is covered with liquid. Cover; simmer for 30 minutes more or till rice is tender. Remove bay leaf. Sprinkle with snipped parsley. Makes 6 servings.

Jollof Rice originated in French colonial Africa. The subtle combination of flavors compares to the chicken jambalaya served in New Orleans homes.

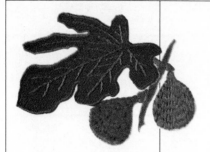

Saudi Arabia

The Bedouin desert tribesmen of Saudi Arabia say, "One's eating shows one's love", and their hospitality is famous; no traveler is ever turned away at mealtime. Bedouin lamb and rice dishes are often served in a single large bowl. With his right hand, each diner tears off a bit of lamb and presses rice around it to make a compact bite.

Sheep and goats thrive on the skimpy grass of this dry area, and provide most of the meat sold in city stores, as well. Eggplant, rice or bulgur, and beans or lentils often accompany the lamb. Sesame and olive oils are used in cooking and add distinctive flavor. Sweets are loved here for snacks and desserts. The sweetening comes from honey or sugar syrup and the treats may be perfumed with fragrant orange flower water or rose water.

GREEN BEANS AND SHRIMP

8 ounces fresh or frozen
    shelled shrimp
1 pound green beans, cut
    French style
1 large onion, thinly sliced
2 tablespoons cooking oil
¼ cup tomato sauce
¾ teaspoon salt
¼ teaspoon ground coriander
¼ teaspoon ground cinnamon
⅛ teaspoon ground cumin
    Dash pepper
2 medium tomatoes, cut into
    thin wedges

Thaw shrimp, if frozen; cut in half lengthwise. Cook beans, covered, in small amount of boiling *salted water* for about 10 minutes or till crisp-tender; drain. In 10-inch skillet cook onion in hot oil till tender but not brown. Stir in drained beans, shrimp, tomato sauce, salt, coriander, cinnamon, cumin, and pepper. Cook, covered, 3 to 5 minutes or till shrimp turn pink, stirring twice. Add tomato wedges and cook 2 minutes more till heated through, stirring once. Makes 6 servings.

نجاة باوزير

*Nagat M. S. Bawazeer
Jedda, Saudi Arabia*

PITA BREAD

The classic Arabian pocket bread--

1 package active dry yeast
3¼ to 3¾ cups all-purpose flour
¼ cup shortening
1½ teaspoons salt

In large mixer bowl soften yeast in 1¼ cups warm *water* (110° to 115°). Add *2 cups* of the flour, shortening, and salt. Beat at low speed of electric mixer for ½ minute, scraping bowl. Beat 3 minutes at high speed. Stir in as much remaining flour as you can mix in with a spoon. Turn out onto lightly floured surface. Knead in enough remaining flour to make a moderately soft dough that is smooth and elastic (3 to 5 minutes). Cover; let rest in warm place about 15 minutes. Divide into 12 equal portions. Roll each between floured hands into a very smooth ball. Cover with a damp cloth; let rest 10 minutes. Using fingers, gently flatten balls. Cover; let rest 10 minutes. (Keep dough pieces covered till ready to use.)

On well-floured surface lightly roll one piece of dough at a time into a circle 7 inches in diameter, *turning dough over once.* Do not stretch, puncture, or crease dough. (Work with enough flour so dough does not stick.) Place on a baking sheet. Bake rounds, 2 at time, in a 450° oven about 3 minutes or till dough is puffed and softly set. Turn over with a spatula; bake about 2 minutes more or till dough is light brown. Repeat with remaining dough, baking one batch before rolling and baking the next batch. To serve, slice bread crosswise; fill pocket with desired filling. Makes 12 rounds.

MACARONI WITH TOMATO-ALMOND SAUCE

    4 ounces elbow macaroni
    1 medium onion, thinly sliced
    2 tablespoons butter or
        margarine
 ⅔ cup water
    2 tablespoons tomato paste
    2 tablespoons finely chopped
        almonds
    1 tablespoon dried chopped
        shrimp
 ½ teaspoon salt
 ¼ teaspoon ground cinnamon
 ⅛ teaspoon ground ginger
 ⅛ teaspoon fennel seed
    1 large tomato, cut up
    1 hard-cooked egg, sliced
    1 lemon, cut into wedges
        Parsley

Cook the macaroni in boiling *salted water* till tender; drain. Meanwhile, in skillet cook onion in butter or margarine till tender but not brown. Add the ⅔ cup water, tomato paste, almonds, shrimp, salt, cinnamon, ginger, fennel, and tomato. Bring to boiling. Cook, uncovered, over medium heat for 5 minutes, stirring occasionally. Place drained macaroni on large plate; spoon sauce atop. Garnish with egg slices, lemon wedges, and parsley. Serves 4.

Samira M. Dajlan
Mecca, Saudi Arabia

FIGS IN SYRUP

Figs grow well in Arabia and are a popular dessert, plain or dressed up like this--

 ½ lemon
 ¼ cup sugar
    2 tablespoons honey
    1 whole clove
 18 walnut halves
 18 fresh figs or one 17-ounce
        jar whole figs, drained
 ½ cup plain yogurt
 ¼ teaspoon vanilla
        Chopped walnuts

With vegetable peeler, cut a thin strip of peel about 2 inches long from lemon. Set aside. Squeeze juice from lemon; add *water* to measure ½ cup. Combine lemon peel strip, lemon juice mixture, sugar, honey, and clove. Bring to boilng; reduce heat. Cook and stir till syrup is thickened and bubbly. Remove from heat; discard clove and lemon peel. Cool slightly. Insert one walnut half into each fig. Place in individual dessert dishes. Stir together cooled syrup, yogurt, and vanilla; spoon over figs. Cover; chill till serving time. Sprinkle with chopped walnuts. Makes 6 servings.

LATIN

AMERICA

Venezuela

Meat is served at nearly every meal in Latin America. But unlike North American beef which is grain-fed and well marbled with fat, Latin American cattle are grass fed, producing lean and less-tender meat cuts. To guarantee flavor and tenderness, Venezuelan cooks employ creative cooking methods. Cutting meat into small pieces and marinating or simmering it in zesty sauces with a generous variety of locally grown vegetables and fruits are typical techniques used in Venezuelan cooking. Many recipes include lard, bacon, or sausages as well as herbs and spices to season meat dishes. The recipe for Venezuelan Beef Stew at right is a good example of this cooking style.

BEEF STEW

5 slices bacon, cut up
1 pound beef round steak
¼ cup all-purpose flour
4 ounces fully cooked ham, cubed (¾ cup)
2½ ounces small smoked sausage links
1 4-ounce package sliced pepperoni
1 14½-ounce can tomatoes, cut up
½ cup chopped green pepper
¼ cup chopped celery
1 cup beef broth
¼ cup dry sherry
1½ teaspoons snipped cilantro
1½ teaspoons steak sauce
1½ teaspoons Worcestershire sauce
⅛ teaspoon dry mustard
Dash ground cloves
1½ cups cubed, peeled potato
1 cup tiny frozen onions
½ cup sliced carrot
1 cup frozen peas

In a Dutch oven cook bacon till crisp; drain bacon and set aside. Reserve drippings in Dutch oven. Trim off fatty edges from round steak. Cut meat into 1-inch cubes; toss with enough flour to coat.

Brown meat in the hot drippings. Drain off fat; stir in next 13 ingredients. Bring to boiling; reduce heat. Cover; simmer 1 hour or till meat is nearly tender. Add potatoes, onions, and carrots. Cover; cook 25 to 35 minutes more, adding peas last 5 minutes. Skim off fat, if necessary. Sprinkle with bacon. Serves 10.

Maritza De Padron
Maracaibo, Venezuela

BAKED SNAPPER FILLETS

2 tablespoons chopped onion
2 tablespoons chopped parsley
4 red snapper fillets or other fish fillets, skinned (about 1 pound)
2 tablespoons butter or margarine
2 tablespoons all-purpose flour
⅛ teaspoon salt
1 cup milk
1 4-ounce can sliced mushrooms, drained
¼ cup dry sherry
¼ cup grated Parmesan cheese
Paprika or snipped chives

Sprinkle onion and parsley in bottom of 12x7½x2-inch baking dish. Arrange fish fillets in dish. Cover; bake in a 350° oven for 30 minutes or till fish flakes easily when tested with a fork. Drain off any liquid that has accumulated in baking dish.

Meanwhile, in a saucepan melt butter. Stir in flour till blended. Add milk all at once. Stir in mushrooms. Cook and stir till thickened and bubbly. Cook and stir 1 to 2 minutes more. Stir in sherry. Pour over fish. Sprinkle with Parmesan cheese. Return to oven and bake, uncovered, about 5 minutes more or till heated through. Sprinkle with paprika or chives. Makes 4 servings.

Luisa De Marin
Boca del Rio, Venezuela

THREE-WAY CHEESE BALL

1 8-ounce package cream
  cheese
4 cups shredded cheddar
  cheese
2 tablespoons milk
2 tablespoons grated onion
2 tablespoons Worcestershire
  sauce
½ cup crumbled blue cheese
¾ teaspoon garlic powder
¼ cup snipped parsley
2 tablespoons chopped
  pecans
2 teaspoons cracked black
  pepper

Let cream cheese and cheddar cheese stand at room temperature till softened. In mixer bowl combine cheeses, onion, milk, and Worcestershire; beat with electric mixer till fluffy. Divide mixture into thirds, about 1 cup each. To one portion beat in blue cheese; to a second portion stir in the garlic powder. Shape each portion into a ball; chill 30 minutes till slightly firm.

Roll the blue cheese ball in snipped parsley. Roll the garlic cheese ball in the chopped pecans. Roll the plain cheese ball in black pepper. Chill at least 1 hour more till cheese balls are firm. Serve with crisp crackers. Makes 3 cheese balls.

Josefina de Fernandez
Caracas, Venezuela

Three-Way Cheese Ball offers robust flavor combinations to please anyone's taste. Choose from black pepper and cheddar cheese, snipped parsley and blue cheese, or pecans and garlic cheese.

Mexico

Griddle-hot corn or flour tortillas are an absolute basic in Mexican cookery. The famous tortilla is used by Mexican cooks in many interesting ways. Wrapped around a variety of fillings, like shredded meat, chicken, seafood, or cheese, a tortilla can become a taco, an enchilada, a burrito, chimichanga, or flauta.

Large tortillas are also fried flat till crisp, sprinkled with shredded cheese, vegetables, and seasoned cooked meat to make salad-like tostados.

Nachos are crisp pieces of corn tortillas (or purchased corn chips) topped with cheese and hot chili peppers and served hot as a snack or party appetizer.

ROLLED SHRIMP CANAPÉS

1 pound fresh or frozen
    medium shrimp in shells
10 slices bacon
½ of a 3-ounce package cream
    cheese with chives,
    softened
2 teaspoons lemon juice
    Dash bottled hot pepper
    sauce

Thaw shrimp, if frozen. Remove shells and devein. Cut bacon slices in half crosswise. In a skillet cook bacon about 4 minutes or till partially cooked; remove bacon to absorbent paper toweling. Split shrimp in half lengthwise; spread one half of each shrimp with *½ teaspoon* of the softened cream cheese; replace top half of shrimp.

Combine lemon juice and hot pepper sauce. Brush each stuffed shrimp with some of the lemon mixture. Wrap each stuffed shrimp, about ½ inch from top (head) end, with one of the bacon halves. Secure each with a wooden pick. To broil, place on an unheated broiler rack and broil 4 to 5 inches from heat for 2 to 3 minutes. Turn. Broil 2 minutes more or till shrimp are done. Serve hot. Makes 16 to 20 appetizers.

*Josefina Campos Ramirez
Veracruz, Mexico*

CRACKLING SALAD

A colorful chilled cactus salad with bits of bacon and hot peppers--

¼ pound sliced bacon
1 15-ounce jar pickled cactus,
    drained, rinsed, and
    cut into ½-inch strips
    (1⅔ cups)
2 medium fresh tomatoes,
    cored and chopped
1 medium onion, chopped
    (½ cup)
1 to 2 tablespoons chopped
    and seeded pickled
    jalapeño strips, or chopped
    pickled serrano chilies
1½ teaspoons snipped fresh
    oregano or ½ teaspoon
    dried oregano, crushed
1 medium avocado, peeled,
    pitted, and sliced

Cut bacon into 1-inch pieces. Cook bacon till crisp; drain on absorbent paper toweling. Cover and chill.

In a mixing bowl stir together cactus strips, chopped tomatoes, chopped onion, and jalapeño strips or green chilies. Stir in oregano. Cover and chill several hours. To serve, arrange avocado slices atop cactus salad and sprinkle with crumbled bacon. Makes 5 or 6 servings.

*Susana de Nova
Federal District, Mexico*

Colorful Fish Veracruz, named for the beautiful port city of Veracruz, is simmered in a sophisticated sauce of tomatoes, garlic, parsley, fresh mint and thyme, jalapeño peppers, and capers. (See recipe, page 18.)

Mexico

FISH VERACRUZ

Pictured on page 17--

> 2 pounds fresh or frozen red snapper or cod fillets
> 2 tablespoons lemon juice
> 1 pound tomatoes, cored, seeded, and finely chopped (3 cups)
> 1½ cups chopped onions
> 2 cloves garlic, minced
> 1 tablespoon snipped parsley
> 1 tablespoon snipped fresh mint
> 3 tablespoons olive oil
> 1 small jalapeño pepper, rinsed, seeded, and cut into strips
> ¼ cup sliced pimiento-stuffed olives
> 1 tablespoon capers
> 1 bay leaf
> 1 tablespoon snipped fresh thyme

Thaw fish, if frozen. Sprinkle with some *salt* and drizzle with the lemon juice; set aside. In a 12-inch skillet cook chopped tomatoes, onions, garlic, parsley, and mint in hot oil till onion is tender but not brown. Add jalapeño pepper strips, olives, capers, bay leaf, and thyme. Heat to boiling. Add fish. Cover; simmer 10 to 15 minutes or till fish flakes easily when tested with a fork.

Transfer fish and vegetables to platter; keep warm. Discard bay leaf. Boil cooking liquid, uncovered, 3 minutes or till reduced to *½ cup.* Pour over fish and vegetables. Garnish with parsley, capers, and tomato, if desired. Serves 6 to 8.

Ana Maria Gonzalez Morales
Veracruz, Mexico

MEXICAN CHOCOLATE CAKE

Chocolate and vanilla are popular flavorings in Mexican desserts--

> ½ cup butter or margarine
> 2 cups packed brown sugar
> 2 eggs
> 1 teaspoon vanilla
> 6 squares (6 ounces) unsweetened chocolate, grated
> 2 cups all-purpose flour
> 1 teaspoon baking soda
> 1¼ cups milk
> Creamy Chocolate Frosting

In a large mixer bowl beat the butter or margarine for 30 seconds till light. Gradually add the brown sugar, beating till well mixed. Add the eggs, one at a time, beating well after each addition. Beat in vanilla and grated chocolate.

In a mixing bowl combine flour and baking soda; add alternately with the milk to beaten butter-chocolate mixture. Turn batter into greased and floured 13x9x2-inch baking pan. Bake in a 350° oven for 35 to 40 minutes or till cake tests done. Cool completely on a wire rack. Frost with your favorite creamy chocolate frosting.

Maria de los Angeles Corona
Morelia, Mexico

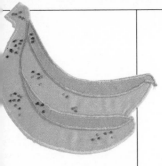

Guatemala & Honduras

Succulent, fresh fruits are plentiful in Latin America. A common sight is the colorful fruit stand that provides a bright and lavish display of the many native fruits. Among the familiar bananas, melons, pineapples, citrus fruits, and coconuts, are exotic tropical fruits such as tender mangoes, guavas, and papayas.

In Guatemala and Honduras, fresh fruit is an indispensable part of the diet for every family. With banana and papaya trees growing by your door, it's as economical and practical as it is delicious. Because fruit is as versatile as it is plentiful, its possiblities in cooking are endless. Enjoyed plain or in frothy drinks, delicate soups, moist breads, crisp golden fritters, or creamy puddings, fresh fruits exemplify the delicious food heritage of Latin America.

SPICY MEATBALL SOUP

2 hard-cooked eggs
½ cup cooked brown rice
¼ cup soft bread crumbs
¼ cup chopped green onion
¼ cup chopped pitted
    ripe olives
¼ teaspoon dried rosemary,
    crushed
    Dash ground cloves
    Dash ground cinnamon
½ pound ground beef
½ pound ground pork
    Raisins
2 cups beef broth
1 10¾-ounce can condensed
    tomato soup
1 tablespoon chili powder
½ cup shredded Monterey Jack
    cheese (2 ounces)
    Coarsely chopped pitted ripe
    olives (optional)
    Chopped green onion
    (optional)

Separate egg yolks from egg whites. Chop each separately. In a bowl combine the egg yolks, rice, bread crumbs, the ¼ cup green onion, the ¼ cup ripe olives, the rosemary, cloves, and cinnamon. Add ground beef and pork; mix well. Using *1½ tablespoons* meat mixture for each meatball, wrap mixture around *two or three* raisins and shape into balls.

In a large saucepan combine beef broth, condensed tomato soup, chili powder, and meatballs. Bring to boiling; reduce heat. Cover and simmer for 30 minutes. Stir in chopped egg whites. Top each serving with some of the cheese, and additional olives and chopped green onion, if desired. Makes 4 to 6 servings.

BREAD AND WINE DESSERT

The character of this aromatic dessert will vary depending upon the type of wine you choose. A dry red wine such as Burgundy or Chianti creates a mellow flavor, while a sweet red wine like Marsala imparts a delicate sweetness--

2 beaten eggs
¼ cup red wine
6 ¾-inch-thick slices French
    bread
2 tablespoons butter or
    margarine
½ cup raisins
⅓ cup red wine
¼ cup honey
¼ teaspoon ground cloves
    Sifted powdered sugar

In shallow dish combine eggs and the ¼ cup wine. Dip bread slices in egg mixture. In a 10-inch skillet cook bread in hot butter on both sides till golden brown. Remove bread and set aside.

In the same skillet stir together raisins, the ⅓ cup red wine, the honey, and cloves. Return bread to skillet. Cover and cook over low heat 15 minutes. Invert bread slices into individual serving bowls and spoon wine sauce atop. Sprinkle each serving with powdered sugar. Makes 6 servings.

Argentina & Uruguay

When you look for a special character in the foods on dinner tables in Argentina or Uruguay, you'll note the Indian influence. Indian cooking styles, combined with those of the early European settler, have evolved into a unique cuisine.

The most ancient of Indian crops are the squash and pumpkin. These nutritious and widely available vegetables are used to prepare interesting dishes such as baked squash pudding, much like a crustless pie, and squash soup. Colorful "carbonada criolla," a classic Argentine dish, makes creative use of a pumpkin by scooping out the seeds and then filling it with a mixture of beef, corn, and peaches. The strong-shelled vegetable doubles as a baking "dish" for this hearty stew.

APPLE DESSERT

3 cups self-rising flour
2 cups sugar
1 cup shortening
1 teaspoon finely shredded lemon peel
4 medium cooking apples, peeled, cored, and sliced (3 cups)
1 cup warm milk
2 eggs
¼ cup brandy or whiskey
1 teaspoon vanilla
    Vanilla ice cream or whipped cream (optional)

Grease and flour a 13x9x2-inch baking pan; set aside.

In a mixing bowl stir together the flour and sugar; cut in shortening till mixture resembles coarse crumbs. Stir in lemon peel. Place *half* of the crumb mixture in bottom of prepared baking pan. Cover with *half* of the sliced apples. Top with the remaining crumb mixture, then remaining apples.

Beat together warm milk, eggs, brandy, and vanilla. Pour over apple mixture in baking pan. Bake in 350° oven about 1 hour or till golden and cake tests done. Cool on wire rack 15 to 20 minutes before serving. Cut into squares and serve with scoops of ice cream or dollops of whipped cream, if desired. Makes 12 servings.

Alba Rosa Diaz de Sosa
Quilmes, Argentina

BACON-PEPPERONI BREAD

½ pound sliced bacon
1 4-ounce package sliced pepperoni (1 cup)
5½ to 6 cups all-purpose flour
1 package active dry yeast
½ teaspoon paprika
2 cups warm water (115° to 120°)

In a skillet cook bacon till browned. Drain well on paper toweling; crumble and set aside. Finely chop the pepperoni; set aside.

In a large mixer bowl combine *2 cups* of the all-purpose flour, the yeast, paprika, ¼ teaspoon *salt,* and ⅛ teaspoon *pepper.* Add warm water. Beat at low speed of electric mixer for ½ minute, scraping sides of bowl constantly. Beat 3 minutes at high speed. Stir in bacon and pepperoni. Stir in as much remaining flour as you can mix in with a spoon. Turn out onto a lightly floured surface. Knead in enough remaining flour to make a moderately stiff dough that is smooth and elastic (6 to 8 minutes total). Shape into a ball. Place dough in a lightly greased bowl; turn once to grease surface. Cover; let rise in warm place till double (45 to 60 minutes).

Punch dough down; turn out onto a lightly floured surface. Cover; let rest 10 minutes. Shape into loaf; place in 2 greased 8x4x2-inch loaf pans. Cover; let rise till nearly double (30 to 45 minutes). Bake in a 400° oven about 35 minutes or till done. Remove from pans; cool on wire rack. Makes 2 loaves.

Josefina de Sergi
Capital Federal, Argentina

FRUIT SALAD

2 medium oranges, peeled and
    sectioned
2 medium apples, cored and
    cut into chunks
4 cups shredded lettuce
½ cup chopped celery
2 medium bananas, sliced
1 cup broken pecans
1 cup halved cherry tomatoes
⅓ cup mayonnaise
¼ cup whipping cream
2 tablespoons prepared
    mustard
¼ teaspoon celery seed

In a mixing bowl toss together the
oranges and apples. Cover and chill.
Combine the shredded lettuce and
celery in lettuce-lined serving bowl.
Cover and chill.

At serving time, toss fruit mixture with sliced bananas. Transfer
fruit mixture with a slotted spoon to
the lettuce-lined serving bowl, ar-
ranging evenly over shredded lettuce mixture. Sprinkle pecans atop.
Arrange tomato halves atop salad.
Garnish with celery leaves and cherry tomato rose, if desired.

For dressing, combine mayonnaise, whipping cream, mustard, and
celery seed. Pour over fruit mixture
and toss gently to coat ingredients.
Makes 8 to 10 servings.

Violeta Comodo
Quilmes, Argentina

*Try this refreshing combination of
juicy fruit and crunchy vegetables.
Tossed with a zesty mustard-
whipping cream dressing, easy-to-fix
Fruit Salad is reminiscent of the
classic Waldorf Salad.*

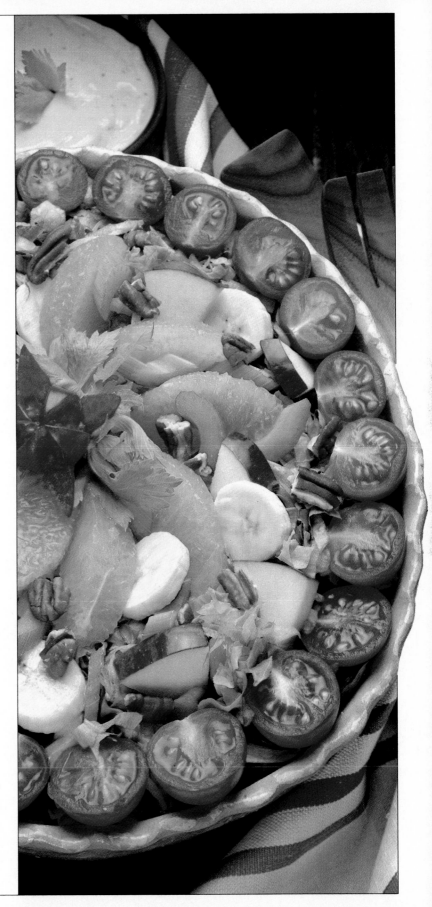

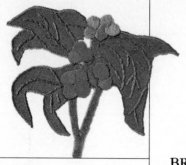

Brazil

Beans are a dietary staple food to the Brazilians, along with rice and manioc (cassava). Beans, especially the small, shiny black ones, are so popular that the national dish, originally created in Rio de Janeiro, is Feijoada Bean Stew. Brazilians love colorful festivities, and this meaty black bean stew appears at many celebrations throughout the year. A more elaborate version of this dish, "Feijoada Completa," is an exuberant mixture of black beans, as many as 15 different meats and vegetables, and numerous garnishes. Several platters are needed to serve this one-dish banquet.

BRIGADEIROS

The Portuguese influence in Brazil is apparent in their many candy and dessert recipes. Portuguese nuns and black slave women were known for preparing tempting sweets rolled in eye-catching coatings and presented in intricate paper doilies. Today, these sugary treats are held in dainty paper cups--

  1 14½-ounce can sweetened condensed milk (1⅓ cups)
  ¼ cup unsweetened cocoa powder
  1 tablespoon butter or margarine
  6 to 8 tablespoons chocolate-flavored sprinkles
    Small foil or paper decorator cups

In a 2-quart saucepan combine condensed milk, cocoa powder, and butter. Cook and stir constantly over medium-low heat 7 to 8 minutes or till candy forms a ball around the spoon and pulls away from the sides of the pan. Cool to room temperature.

With buttered hands, shape cocoa mixture into 1-inch balls; gently roll each in chocolate sprinkles. Place in individual decorator cups. Cover and chill before serving. Refrigerate remaining candies. Makes 25.

*Laides Miguel Da Silva
Bauru, Brazil*

HONEY-SPICE BREAD

  ⅓ cup milk
  ⅔ cup packed brown sugar
  2 cups all-purpose flour
  1½ teaspoons baking powder
  ½ teaspoon ground cinnamon
  ½ teaspoon ground nutmeg
  ⅛ teaspoon ground cloves
  ½ cup honey
  2 eggs, beaten
  ⅓ cup cooking oil
  ⅓ cup sifted powdered sugar (optional)
  1 to 2 teaspoons milk (optional)
    Candied fruit (optional)

In medium saucepan combine milk and brown sugar. Cook and stir over low heat till sugar is dissolved. In bowl stir together flour, baking powder, cinnamon, nutmeg, and cloves. Gradually blend in the milk mixture, the honey, eggs, and cooking oil. Turn batter into a greased and floured 8x4x2-inch loaf pan.

Bake in 350° oven 55 to 60 minutes or till done, covering with foil the last 15 minutes. Cool in pan 10 minutes. Remove from pan; cool thoroughly. If desired, combine powdered sugar and enough milk to make of spreading consistency; frost cooled loaf. Decorate with candied fruit. Makes 1 loaf.

*Rosa C. Negreiros
Cachoeirinha, Brazil*

Honey-Spice Bread gets its golden color from honey, brown sugar, and fragrant spices. Frost the loaf with the powdered sugar icing and decorate with candied fruits or spread thin slices with softened butter or whipped cream cheese.

Paraguay

Paraguay is a land of food surprises. Pasta, introduced by Italian immigrants, is very popular in this South American country. Though Paraguay is far from the sea, fish is a mainstay entrée, with lake and river fish substituting for salt-water varieties. Orange trees flourish in the tropical climate, and the colorful fruit fills the markets. Many families pick fresh oranges from their own trees, since an old law once required each homeowner to plant orange trees in his garden.

The Paraguayan national drink is maté. This refreshing tealike beverage is made from the leaves of a wild shrub. Traditionally it's served hot or cold in a small decorated gourd with a wooden or metal straw.

CHEESE PIE

1 cup all-purpose flour
½ cup cornstarch
½ teaspoon salt
½ cup butter or margarine
¼ cup shredded cheddar cheese
1 beaten egg
3 tablespoons milk
1¾ cups shredded cheddar cheese
½ cup drained cottage cheese
½ cup milk
1 tablespoon all-purpose flour
3 hard-cooked eggs, sliced

In bowl stir together flour, cornstarch, and salt. Cut in butter or margarine till crumbly. Stir in ¼ cup shredded cheese. Combine egg and 3 tablespoons milk; add to flour mixture, stirring till well mixed. Form dough into a ball. On lightly floured surface roll out about ⅔ of dough to 13-inch circle. Ease pastry into 10-inch pie plate, being careful not to stretch pastry. Combine 1¾ cups shredded cheese, cottage cheese, ½ cup milk, and flour. Arrange egg slices in pastry; top with cheese mixture. Roll out remaining pastry; cut into ½-inch strips. Weave strips atop filling to make lattice top. Flute edge. Bake in 375° oven for 30 minutes or till crust is lightly browned. Let stand 10 minutes before serving. Makes 8 servings.

Maura de Kamm
Asuncion, Paraguay

LAYERED CORN PIE

¾ pound ground beef
1 large onion, chopped
½ cup chopped green pepper
2 cloves garlic, minced
1 large tomato, chopped
¼ cup beef broth
¾ teaspoon cumin
2 hard-cooked eggs, chopped
4 cups fresh cut corn or
    two 10-ounce packages
    frozen corn
2 tablespoons lard or
    shortening, melted
2 medium onions, chopped
3 eggs
1 tablespoon all-purpose flour
1 cup cottage cheese

Cook meat, 1 onion, green pepper, and garlic till meat is browned. Drain off fat. Add tomato, broth, cumin, ½ teaspoon *salt*, and ⅛ teaspoon *pepper;* cook and stir for 5 minutes. Stir in hard-cooked eggs. Place corn, half at a time, in blender container or food processor. Cover; process till finely chopped. (Add milk, if necessary, to make 2½ cups.) Set aside. Cook 2 chopped onions in lard or shortening till tender. Beat together eggs, flour, ¼ teaspoon *salt* and ⅛ teaspoon *pepper.* Stir in cottage cheese, onion mixture, and corn. Place half the corn mixture in greased 12x7½x2-inch baking dish. Top with meat mixture. Pour remaining corn mixture atop. Bake in 375° oven about 30 minutes. Let stand 10 minutes before serving. Makes 8 servings.

Delia Perez Vda. de Martinez
Asuncion, Paraguay

Chile

A "string bean" country, Chile stretches 2,600 miles, sandwiched between the magnificent Andes Mountains and the beautiful Pacific Ocean. Unlike neighboring countries, Chile is geographically limited in food resources. For their diets its people depend upon fresh seafood and beans, which can be grown nearly year round in Chile's mild climate.

A classic dish served here is "porotos granados," which is Indian in origin. This national food makes use of abundant Indian foodstuffs: beans, corn, and squash. The addition of robust garlic and sweet onion is also characteristic of Chilean cooking. The recipe featured at right, Beans Granados, is a delicious blend of these food staples.

BEANS GRANADOS

- ½ pound dry red kidney beans
- 5 cups water
- 4 cups water
- 1 teaspoon salt
- 3 ears fresh corn
- 1 cup chopped onion
- 2 cloves garlic, minced
- 2 tablespoons butter or margarine
- 1 cup ½-inch cubes acorn squash or other winter squash
- ¾ cup condensed beef broth

In a kettle or Dutch oven combine beans with the 5 cups water. Bring to boiling. Reduce heat; simmer 2 minutes. Remove from heat. Cover; let stand 1 hour. (Or, combine the water and beans. Let stand overnight.) Drain beans. Add 4 cups more water. Stir in salt. Bring to boiling. Cover and cook 1 to 1¼ hours or till beans are tender. Drain. Meanwhile remove corn from cob (should have 1½ cups).

In a skillet cook the onion and garlic in the butter or margarine till tender but not brown. Add the cooked beans, corn, squash, and condensed beef broth. Cook, covered, for 10 minutes more or till squash and corn are tender. Makes 4 servings.

Raquel del Valle Ramirez
Santiago, Chile

EMPANADAS

These sturdy, meat-filled turnovers are common to the South American diet--

- ½ pound boneless beef round steak, cut into ¼-inch cubes
- 1 cup chopped onion
- 2 tablespoons cooking oil
- 2 teaspoons all-purpose flour
- ⅛ teaspoon crushed red pepper
- 4 cups all-purpose flour
- 1 cup hot milk
- ¾ cup lard, melted
- 3 tablespoons raisins
- ⅓ cup sliced pimiento-stuffed olives
- 2 hard-cooked eggs, sliced

In a skillet cook the beef and onion in oil about 5 minutes or till meat and onions are tender. Stir in the 2 teaspoons flour, the red pepper, and ¼ teaspoon *salt.* Cover; cool. In a bowl combine the 4 cups flour and ¼ teaspoon *salt.* Stir in the hot milk and melted lard; mix till combined. Work dough with hands till well mixed. Divide dough into 8 portions about 2 inches in diameter.

On a lightly floured surface roll each portion of dough to a 6-inch circle. On half of each circle place *3 tablespoons* of the meat filling, about *1 teaspoon* raisins, some of the olive slices, and a few slices of hard-cooked egg. Fold the remaining half of the dough over filling. Press edges with fingers or tines of fork to seal. Transfer to baking sheets. Bake in a 400° oven for 20 to 25 minutes or till golden. Makes 8 servings.

Patricia Sanchez Correa
Santiago, Chile

NORT

AMERICA

Canada

In Quebec, Canada's largest province, the French influence in cooking includes many fresh products, especially corn, apples, pork, game, seafood, and maple syrup. Typical of French-Canadian cooking are the robust soups. The French word for a hearty soup or stew, chaudière, has been Americanized to chowder, and the thick and hearty split pea soup or cheese soup is served often on American tables, too.

The French Canadians also enjoy meat pies and two of the most famous dishes from this cuisine are "tourtière" and "cipâté" (French-Canadian pot pie). For dessert the French Canadians are likely to choose something flavored with maple syrup or the ever-popular "buche de Noel", a jelly roll cake with chocolate filling. The cake is arranged and decorated to resemble the festive Yule Log of Christmases past.

APPETIZER LOBSTER ROLLS

20 slices very thinly sliced firm-
  textured white bread
8 ounces cream cheese or other
  mild-flavored process
  cheese
2 tablespoons butter or
  margarine
1 5- or 6-ounce can lobster or
  crab, rinsed, drained,
  cartilage removed, and
  broken into pieces, or
  one 4½-ounce can shrimp,
  rinsed, drained, and
  chopped
2 tablespoons snipped parsley
¼ cup butter or margarine,
  melted
  Sesame seeds

Trim crusts from bread. Roll the bread slices to flatten slightly. In a saucepan heat and stir together cheese and the 2 tablespoons butter or margarine till cheese is melted and mixture is smooth. Add lobster, crab, or shrimp, and the parsley. Spread about *1 tablespoon* seafood mixture on each bread slice; roll up. Melt the remaining ¼ cup butter or margarine; brush over rolls. Sprinkle with sesame seeds. Cut rolls crosswise into thirds. Place on baking sheet. Broil 3 to 4 inches from heat for 3 to 4 minutes or till golden. Makes 60 appetizers.

Theresa Bourassa

Theresa Bourassa
Saskatoon, Saskatchewan

DROP SUGAR COOKIES

2½ cups all-purpose flour
½ teaspoon baking soda
½ teaspoon salt
¼ teaspoon cream of tartar
¼ teaspoon ground nutmeg
  (optional)
1 cup butter or margarine
1 cup sugar
2 eggs
½ teaspoon vanilla
2 cups semisweet chocolate
  pieces; chopped peanuts or
  other nuts; raisins or
  snipped dried apricots; or
  desired combination
  (optional)

In a large mixing bowl stir together the flour, baking soda, salt, cream of tartar, and nutmeg; set aside. In a large mixer bowl beat butter or margarine with electric mixer for 30 seconds. Add sugar and beat till fluffy. Add eggs and vanilla; beat well. Gradually add dry ingredients to beaten mixture, beating well after each addition. Stir in chocolate pieces, nuts, or fruit, if desired. Drop sugar cookie dough from a teaspoon 2 inches apart onto a greased cookie sheet. Bake in a 375° oven for 10 minutes or till edges are golden; cool on a wire rack. Makes about 5 dozen cookies.

Carol Rideout

Carol Rideout
Edmonton, Alberta

STOVE-TOP MEATBALLS

1 beaten egg
⅓ cup milk or water
1 cup soft bread crumbs
1 large onion, finely chopped
1 large clove garlic, minced
½ cup grated Parmesan chesse
½ cup snipped parsley
1 pound ground beef
½ pound ground pork
½ pound ground veal
1 tablespoon cooking oil
1 28-ounce can tomatoes,
   cut up
1 10¾-ounce can tomato puree
1 large onion, chopped
1 clove garlic, minced
1 teaspoon sugar
  Hot cooked noodles
  Grated Parmesan cheese

In a large mixing bowl stir together egg, milk or water, bread crumbs, the finely chopped onion, the 1 clove minced garlic, the ½ cup Parmesan cheese, and the parsley. Add ground beef, pork, and veal; mix well. Shape meat mixture into thirty-two 2-inch meatballs. In a large skillet or Dutch oven brown the meatballs, half at a time, in hot oil. Remove from skillet; pour off drippings. Stir in *undrained* cut-up tomatoes, the tomato puree, the remaining chopped onion, remaining minced garlic, and the sugar. Cook and stir till bubbly. Add meatballs. Cover and simmer 25 to 30 minutes. Serve with hot cooked noodles. Pass additional grated Parmesan cheese to sprinkle atop. Makes 8 servings.

Barb Westwood
Zephyr, Ontario

RHUBARB UPSIDE-DOWN CAKE

2 tablespoons butter or
   margarine
½ cup packed brown sugar
2 cups sliced fresh or
   frozen rhubarb
1½ cups all-purpose flour
2½ teaspoons baking powder
½ teaspoon salt
⅓ cup shortening
¾ cup granulated sugar
1 egg
1½ teaspoons vanilla
⅔ cup milk

Melt the butter or margarine in a 9x1½-inch round baking pan. Stir in brown sugar. Arrange sliced rhubarb in pan. Combine flour, baking powder, and salt. In small mixer bowl beat shortening about 30 seconds. Add granulated sugar; beat till well combined. Add egg and vanilla; beat 1 minute. Add dry ingredients and milk alternately to beaten mixture, beating after each addition. Spread batter evenly over rhubarb. Bake in a 350° oven for 50 to 55 minutes. Cool in pan for 5 minutes; invert onto a serving plate. Serve warm. Makes 8 servings.

Lydia Shantz
Baden, Ontario

Canada

TOURTIÈRE

This hearty French meat pie is as much a part of the French-Canadian Christmas as "Papa Noël" (Santa Claus)--

- 1 pound ground pork
- ½ pound ground veal
- 6 slices bacon, cut up
- ½ cup chopped onion
- ½ cup chopped celery
- 1 clove garlic, minced
- 2 teaspoons dried sage, crushed
- ¼ teaspoon salt
- ¼ teaspoon pepper
- 1¼ cups water
- 2 tablespoons cornstarch
  Pastry for Double-Crust Pie
  (see recipe at right)

In a Dutch oven brown ground pork, ground veal, and bacon pieces. Drain off fat. Stir in chopped onion, chopped celery, garlic, sage, salt, and pepper. Stir in *1 cup* of the water; bring meat-vegetable mixture to boiling. Reduce heat and simmer, covered, for 10 to 15 minutes or till onion is tender, stirring frequently.

Combine cornstarch and the remaining ¼ cup water. Add to hot meat-vegetable mixture, cooking and stirring till thickened and bubbly. Cook and stir 1 to 2 minutes more. Remove pan from heat; cool slightly.

Meanwhile, prepare Pastry for Double-Crust Pie. On a well-floured surface roll out *half* of the pastry to a circle 12 inches in diameter. Fit into a 9-inch pie plate. Trim pastry to ½ inch beyond the edge of the pie plate. Fill pastry shell with meat-vegetable mixture. Roll out remaining pastry to a circle 12 inches in diameter. Make maple leaf cutout, if desired, or cut slits in top crust. Carefully place atop meat filling. Seal and flute pastry edge.

Bake meat pie in a 400° oven about 25 minutes or till golden brown. Let stand 15 minutes before serving. Makes 6 servings.

Pastry for Double-Crust Pie: In a medium mixing bowl stir together 2 cups *all-purpose flour* and 1 teaspoon *salt.* Cut in ⅔ cup *shortening or lard* till the pieces are the size of small peas. Sprinkle 1 tablespoon *cold water* over part of the flour mixture; gently toss with a fork. Push to side of bowl. Repeat with 5 to 6 tablespoons more *cold water* till all is moistened. Form dough into 2 balls.

Cheryle Chagnon

Cheryle Chagnon
Edmonton, Alberta

Wedges of golden, meaty Tourtière are usually served cold at Christmas time after midnight mass.

United States

The stove and refrigerator revolutionized American kitchens before 1940, but since that date a great many convenient and innovative appliances have come to the aid of the homemaker.

More than just a kitchen equipped with only the basics--a gas or electric stove, a refrigerator-freezer, and toaster--a new kitchen has evolved. Today, millions of kitchens boast countless other electric appliances that include the frying pan, blender, mixer, popcorn popper, yogurt maker, coffee maker, microwave oven, dishwasher, and garbage compactor.

FRENCH QUARTER BEAN SOUP

    1 cup dry pinto beans
  ½ cup dry red beans
  ½ cup dry garbanzo beans
    1 to 1½ pounds ham hocks
    2 16-ounce cans tomatoes,
        cut up
  1½ cups chopped celery
    1 cup chopped onion
    2 cloves garlic, minced
    2 bay leaves
  ¼ teaspoon ground red pepper
  ½ pound smoked sausage,
        sliced, cooked, and drained
    1 pound chicken thighs
    3 tablespoons snipped parsley

Rinse beans. In Dutch oven combine beans and enough *water* to cover. Bring to boiling; reduce heat and simmer 2 minutes. Remove from heat. Cover; let stand 1 hour. (Or, soak the beans in water overnight.) Drain; add 6 cups fresh *water* and ham hocks. Bring to boiling; reduce heat. Cover and simmer 1 hour. Remove ham hocks; when cool enough to handle, cut off meat and chop. Discard bones. Return meat to bean mixture. Add *undrained* tomatoes, celery, onion, garlic, bay leaves, and red pepper. Add sliced sausage and chicken thighs. Bring to boiling. Reduce heat; cover and simmer about 1 hour or till chicken and beans are tender. Remove chicken thighs; cool slightly. Remove meat from bones and chop. Discard bones; return meat to soup. Add parsley. Remove bay leaves; discard. Serves 12.

Janet Swoboda
Omaha, Nebraska

CALIFORNIA CHEESE SOUP

Mild-flavored, creamy Monterey Jack cheese originated in California--

  ½ cup chopped onion
    1 clove garlic, minced
  ¼ cup butter or margarine
  ¼ cup all-purpose flour
  ½ teaspoon salt
  ⅛ teaspoon pepper
    3 cups milk
    1 cup chicken broth
    1 cup chopped tomato
  ¼ cup chopped green
        chili peppers
  1½ cups shredded Monterey
        Jack cheese (6 ounces)
    Avocado slices (optional)
    Paprika (optional)

In a 2-quart saucepan cook chopped onion and garlic in butter or margarine till tender. Stir in flour, salt, and pepper. Add milk and chicken broth all at once. Cook and stir over medium heat till slightly thickened and bubbly; cook and stir 1 minute more. Stir in chopped tomato and chopped chili peppers. Add shredded Monterey Jack cheese; cook over low heat till melted, stirring constantly. Garnish each serving with avocado slices and paprika, if desired. Makes 6 servings.

Suzanne Ringler
Oklahoma City, Oklahoma

French Quarter Bean Soup is a hearty bean and sausage chowder reminiscent of the spicy dishes native to the American South. Accompany bowls of the hot soup with slices of crusty French bread or corn bread.

United States

MINI CHEESE TARTS

½ cup butter or margarine, softened
1 3-ounce package cream cheese, softened
1 cup all-purpose flour
½ cup diced fully-cooked ham
⅓ cup shredded Swiss cheese
4 slices bacon, crisp-cooked and crumbled (¼ cup)
2 tablespoons finely chopped onion
2 beaten eggs
½ cup milk
Dash pepper
Dash ground nutmeg

For pastry, in a small mixer bowl beat butter or margarine and softened cream cheese till blended. Add flour; beat well. Cover bowl; chill mixture at least 1 hour. Shape chilled dough into twenty-four 1-inch balls; place each ball in an ungreased 1¾-inch muffin cup. Press dough onto bottom and sides of cups. Chill 30 minutes. Divide ham, cheese, bacon, and onion among pastry-lined cups. Combine eggs, milk, pepper, and nutmeg. Spoon about 2 teaspoons egg mixture into each cup. Bake in 400° oven for 18 to 20 minutes or till lightly browned. Cool 5 minutes before removing from pan. Serve tarts warm or chilled. Makes 24 appetizers.

Claire Brousseau
Danvers, Massachusetts

MARINATED MUSHROOMS AND OLIVES

Serve this colorful appetizer with your favorite Italian-style dinner--

2 cups halved medium fresh mushrooms
1 10-ounce can pitted ripe olives, drained
2 tablespoons snipped parsley
½ cup olive oil or salad oil
¼ cup dry white wine
¼ cup lemon juice
1 small clove garlic, minced
½ teaspoon dried oregano, crushed
¼ teaspoon salt
⅛ teaspoon pepper
1 medium red onion, thinly sliced

In a mixing bowl stir together mushrooms, olives, and parsley. In a screw-top jar combine oil, white wine, lemon juice, garlic, oregano, salt, and pepper; shake well. Pour over mushroom mixture; stir to coat well. Cover and refrigerate overnight or for several days; stir occasionally. Stir in red onion slices just before serving. Makes 4½ cups.

Valjean Araya
Pinole, California

BEER BISCUITS

Self-rising flour speeds the mixing of these flavorful biscuits. Pictured on page 37--

3 slices bacon
  Cooking oil
2 cups self-rising flour
2 teaspoons sugar
⅔ cup beer

In a 12-inch heavy, oven-going skillet cook bacon till crisp; drain, reserving drippings. Add enough oil to the bacon drippings to make ¼ *cup;* set aside. Crumble cooked bacon (should have about ¼ cup). In a mixing bowl combine self-rising flour and sugar. Add the crumbled bacon. Add the bacon drippings and oil mixture and the beer; stir just till combined. Turn dough out onto a lightly floured surface; knead 10 to 12 strokes. Roll or pat dough to a ½-inch thickness. Cut with floured 2½-inch cutter. Arrange in the 12-inch oven-going skillet. Bake in a 450° oven about 12 minutes or till golden brown. Makes 10 biscuits.

  Note: If you don't have a 12-inch heavy, oven-going skillet, fry the bacon slices in a small skillet and bake the biscuits on an ungreased baking sheet.

Cheryl Houser

Cheryl Houser
Broken Arrow, Oklahoma

THREE-WHEAT BATTER BREAD

Healthful ingredients like whole wheat flour, wheat germ, and cracked wheat give home-baked breads a hearty, nutty taste--

2¼ cups all-purpose flour
  1 cup whole wheat flour
  ¼ cup wheat germ
  ¼ cup cracked wheat
  1 package active dry yeast
  ½ teaspoon ground ginger
  1 13-ounce can evaporated
    milk
  3 tablespoons honey
  2 tablespoons cooking oil
  1 teaspoon salt

In a large mixer bowl combine *1 cup* of the all-purpose flour, the whole wheat flour, wheat germ, cracked wheat, yeast, and ginger. In a saucepan heat the milk, honey, oil, and salt just till warm (115° to 120°). Add to flour mixture. Beat at low speed of electric mixer for 30 seconds, scraping sides of bowl constantly. Beat 3 minutes at high speed. Stir in remaining all-purpose flour. Cover batter. Let rise in warm place about 1 hour or till double. Beat down with a wooden spoon. Spoon into 2 greased 1-pound coffee cans. Cover and let rise in warm place for 40 to 45 minutes or till almost double. Bake bread in 350° oven about 40 minutes or till brown. Remove bread from cans and cool thoroughly on a wire rack. Makes 2 loaves.

Chris Linn

Chris Linn
Casper, Wyoming

United States

BROCCOLI-CAULIFLOWER SALAD

3½ cups cauliflower flowerets
3 cups broccoli flowerets
½ cup chopped onion
⅔ cup bottled green goddess dressing
⅓ cup mayonnaise or salad dressing
2 tablespoons vinegar
1 teaspoon celery seed
¼ cup radish slices or 6 cherry tomatoes, halved (optional)

Slice or coarsely chop large pieces of cauliflower and broccoli. In a large bowl combine cauliflower, broccoli, and onion. In another bowl beat together the green goddess salad dressing, mayonnaise or salad dressing, vinegar, and celery seed; pour over vegetables. Toss to coat well. Cover and chill thoroughly. Top salad with radish slices or cherry tomato halves, if desired. Makes 12 servings.

Wanda Fosson

Wanda Fosson
Ashland, Kentucky

MOLDED BUTTERMILK SALAD

Creamy whipped dessert topping, walnuts, and fruit make this a popular luncheon gelatin salad. The buttermilk adds the tang--

1 20-ounce can crushed pineapple
1 6-ounce package strawberry-flavored gelatin
2½ cups buttermilk
1 8-ounce container frozen whipped dessert topping, thawed
¾ cup chopped walnuts
Lettuce
Fresh strawberries (optional)
Pineapple slices (optional)

In a medium saucepan combine *undrained* crushed pineapple and strawberry gelatin. Heat and stir till gelatin dissolves. Cool about 15 minutes. Stir in buttermilk. Chill till mixture is partially thickened. Fold in whipped dessert topping and walnuts. Turn fruit mixture into 8-cup mold. Cover and chill several hours or overnight till firm. Unmold onto a lettuce-lined serving plate. Garnish salad with fresh strawberries and sliced pineapple, if desired. Makes 12 servings.

Nora Lou Ray

Nora Lou Ray
Centre, Alabama

Golden, bacon-flecked Beer Biscuits are crusty on the outside while moist and tender on the inside. Serve them hot from the oven with lots of butter! (See recipe, page 35.)

United States

GARDEN POTATO SALAD

6 medium potatoes (2 pounds)
⅔ cup mayonnaise or
   salad dressing
1 tablespoon prepared
   horseradish
⅛ teaspoon pepper
1 8¼-ounce can sliced carrots,
   drained
¾ cup frozen peas, thawed
½ cup chopped onion
¾ cup chopped dill pickle
1 16-ounce jar pickled sliced
   beets, chilled
   Sliced radish (optional)
   Parsley (optional)

Cook *unpeeled* potatoes in boiling
salted water about 40 minutes or till
tender; drain. Cool, peel, and dice
potatoes. Stir together mayonnaise
or salad dressing, horseradish, and
pepper. In a large mixing bowl
combine the diced potatoes, carrots,
peas, onion, and chopped dill pickle. Add the mayonnaise mixture to
potato mixture; toss lightly to coat
evenly. Cover and chill. Drain and
cut beets into strips; toss with
chilled potato mixture just before
serving. Garnish potato salad with
sliced radish and parsley sprig, if desired. Makes 6 to 8 servings.

Bertha Illemszky
Cape Coral, Florida

HERBED ZUCCHINI

*Garden-fresh zucchini are at their best in this
easy skillet side dish--*

4 slices bacon
½ cup chopped onion
½ cup chopped celery
1 7½-ounce can tomatoes,
   cut up
1 tablespoon snipped parsley
¼ teaspoon dried sage, crushed
¼ teaspoon dried summer
   savory, crushed
¼ teaspoon dried oregano,
   crushed
⅛ teaspoon pepper
3½ cups sliced zucchini
   (3 medium)
⅓ cup grated Parmesan cheese

In a skillet cook bacon till crisp.
Drain bacon, reserving *2 tablespoons*
of the drippings in skillet. Crumble
bacon; set aside.
   Cook chopped onion and celery
in bacon drippings till tender but
not brown. Stir in the *undrained* tomatoes, the parsley, sage, savory,
oregano, and pepper. Add sliced
zucchini. Bring vegetable mixture to
boiling; reduce heat. Cover and
cook about 10 minutes or till zucchini is crisp-tender, stirring occasionally. Sprinkle with Parmesan
cheese and crumbled bacon. Makes
4 to 6 servings.

Betty Nagel
Summerfield, Illinois

WILD RICE SUPREME

This prized grain is really the seed of a marsh grass grown in Minnesota. It is still harvested from boats in much the same way the Sioux and Chippewa Indians did centuries ago--

1 cup uncooked wild rice
   (4½ cups cooked)
4 cups water
1 teaspoon salt
1 pound fresh mushrooms,
   sliced (6 cups)
1 cup chopped onion
½ cup chopped celery
¼ cup butter or margarine
1 10¾-ounce can condensed
   cream of mushroom soup
1 cup whipping cream

In a saucepan with tight-fitting lid combine rice, water, and salt. Bring to boiling. Reduce heat and simmer, covered, for 45 minutes or till tender. Drain well. In a skillet cook the sliced mushrooms, chopped onion, and chopped celery in butter or margarine till tender. In mixing bowl stir together mushroom soup and whipping cream; stir in vegetable mixture and cooked rice. Turn the rice-vegetable mixture into a 2-quart casserole. Bake in a 350° oven for 40 minutes or till heated through. Makes 8 to 10 servings.

Helen Gailfus

Helen Gailfus
Bloomington, Minnesota

Creamy Garden Potato Salad is a colorful combination of cubed potatoes, peas, beets, sliced carrots, onion, and dill pickle. The lively dressing boasts a hint of horseradish.

United States

CHEESE-SCALLOPED CARROTS

6 cups sliced carrots (about 12 medium)
½ cup finely chopped celery
¼ cup finely chopped onion
2 tablespoons butter or margarine
2 tablespoons all-purpose flour
¼ teaspoon salt
¼ teaspoon dry mustard
Dash pepper
1½ cups milk
1 cup shredded cheddar cheese
2 tablespoons snipped parsley
1½ cups soft bread crumbs (2 slices)
2 tablespoons butter or margarine, melted

Cook sliced carrots in boiling salted water about 12 minutes or till just tender. Drain well and set aside; keep warm. For cheese sauce, in a saucepan cook the celery and onion in the 2 tablespoons butter or margarine till tender. Stir in flour, salt, mustard, and pepper. Add milk all at once. Cook and stir over medium heat till thickened and bubbly. Cook and stir 1 minute more. Stir in the shredded cheddar cheese and parsley till the cheese is melted. Place the drained, cooked carrots in a 1½-quart casserole. Pour cheese sauce over carrots. Stir gently to mix. Toss together the bread crumbs and melted 2 tablespoons butter; sprinkle over carrot-cheese mixture. Bake in a 350° oven for 25 minutes or till heated through. Makes 8 servings.

Diane Dobbs
Decatur, Illinois

HASH BROWN POTATO CASSEROLE

Fried hash brown potatoes are an American favorite. Try this hearty variation--

2 cups shredded American or cheddar cheese (8 ounces)
1 10¾-ounce can condensed cream of chicken soup
1 cup dairy sour cream
½ cup finely chopped onion
¼ cup butter or margarine, melted
¼ teaspoon salt
¼ teaspoon pepper
1 32-ounce package frozen loose-pack hash brown potatoes, thawed
1 cup crushed cornflakes
1 tablespoon butter or margarine, melted

Grease a 13x9x2-inch baking dish; set aside. In a large mixing bowl combine shredded cheese, chicken soup, sour cream, chopped onion, the ¼ cup melted butter or margarine, salt, and pepper. Mix well. Fold in thawed hash brown potatoes. Turn the potato-cheese mixture into prepared baking dish. Toss together the cornflakes and 1 tablespoon melted butter or margarine; sprinkle over potato mixture. Bake in a 350° oven about 1 hour or till casserole is golden and potatoes are tender. Makes 8 to 10 servings.

Betty Miller
Madison, Wisconsin

Hunter-Style Chicken teams tender pieces of chicken with the robust flavors of garlic, fresh mushrooms, white wine, and garden-fresh tomatoes for a tasty oven-baked entrée. (See recipe, page 42.)

United States

BROCCOLI-RICE CASSEROLE

Take this popular covered dish to your next potluck gathering--

2 10-ounce packages frozen
    chopped broccoli
¼ cup chopped onion
1 10¾-ounce can condensed
    cream of chicken soup
½ cup milk
¼ cup water
2 cups shredded cheddar
    cheese (8 ounces)
1 cup quick-cooking rice

In saucepan cook broccoli and onion in boiling salted water for 5 minutes; drain well. In bowl thoroughly mix cream of chicken soup, milk, water, and shredded cheese. Stir in *uncooked* rice and the drained broccoli-onion mixture. Turn into 2-quart casserole. Bake, uncovered, in a 350° oven for 45 minutes, stirring once. Let stand 10 minutes before serving. Makes 10 to 12 servings.

Tina Camden

Tina Camden
Manteca, California

HUNTER-STYLE CHICKEN

Pictured on page 41--

2 tablespoons butter
2 tablespoons cooking oil
4 chicken breasts, split
    lengthwise, skinned and
    boned (2 pounds boneless)
1 cup sliced onions
1 cup sliced fresh mushrooms
1 clove garlic, minced
3 tablespoons all-purpose flour
½ teaspoon salt
⅛ teaspoon pepper
1 cup dry white wine
1 cup chicken broth
1 cup diced tomatoes
¼ cup snipped parsley
    Hot cooked rice or noodles

In a large skillet heat together butter and oil. Cook chicken pieces over medium heat about 25 minutes, turning to brown. Remove chicken to a 12x7½x2-inch baking dish; keep warm.

For vegetable sauce, in the same skillet combine onion, mushrooms, and garlic. Cook and stir till onion is tender. Stir in flour, salt, and pepper; mix well. Add wine, chicken broth, and tomatoes; mix well. Cook and stir over medium high heat until mixture is thickened and bubbly; cook and stir 1 minute more. Pour vegetable sauce over chicken in dish. Bake, uncovered, in a 350° oven for 30 minutes or till chicken is tender. Sprinkle with snipped parsley. Garnish with tomato wedges and parsley, if desired. Serve with hot cooked rice or noodles. Makes 6 to 8 servings.

Betty Urbanek

Betty Urbanek
Andrews, Texas

SOUTHWESTERN POCKET SANDWICHES

These spicy pita sandwiches (much like a taco) are great for both meals and snacks--

1 pound ground beef
½ cup chopped onion
1 1¼-ounce package taco
   seasoning mix
1 cup water
1 8¼-ounce can refried beans
4 pita bread rounds (5½-inch
   diameter), halved
   crosswise (recipe page 10)
¾ cup shredded cheddar cheese
   (3 ounces)
1 cup shredded lettuce
1 small tomato, chopped
   Taco sauce

In a skillet cook ground beef and chopped onion till meat is brown and onion is tender; drain off excess fat. Add taco seasoning mix and water; bring mixture to boiling. Reduce heat; simmer 15 minutes. Stir in refried beans. Spoon about *¼ cup* of the bean mixture into each pita bread round half. Place, open side up, in a 10x6x2-inch baking dish. Top each with some of the shredded cheddar cheese. Bake, uncovered, in a 375° oven for 20 minutes. Top each pita bread round with some shredded lettuce and chopped tomato. Pass taco sauce to pour over each. Makes 4 servings.

Judy Wilson
Lake Havasu City, Arizona

FISH FLORENTINE

2 pounds fresh or frozen
   flounder fillets (8 fillets)
1 10-ounce package frozen
   chopped spinach, thawed
   and well drained
1 cup cooked rice
¼ cup sliced green onion
¼ cup toasted slivered almonds
¼ teaspoon salt
⅛ teaspoon ground nutmeg
   Dash pepper
1 10¾-ounce can condensed
   cream of mushroom soup
½ cup milk
1 tablespooon lemon juice
   Paprika
   Toasted slivered almonds
   (optional)

Thaw fish fillets, if frozen. If fillets are in pieces, press fish together to form 8 whole fillets. In mixing bowl combine spinach, rice, onion, the ¼ cup almonds, salt, nutmeg, and pepper. Place about *¼ cup* filling near wide end of each fillet; fold narrow end over filling. Place in a greased 12x7½x2-inch baking dish. Stir together mushroom soup, milk, and lemon juice; spoon evenly over fish.

Bake, uncovered, in a 400° oven about 30 minutes or till fish flakes easily when tested with a fork. Spoon mushroom sauce over fillets to serve. Sprinkle with paprika. If desired, sprinkle with additional toasted almonds. Makes 8 servings.

Debra Chansky
Medford, New York

United States

PASTA PIZZA SQUARES

8 ounces lasagna noodles
1 pound bulk Italian sausage
2 cups shredded mozzarella
  cheese (8 ounces)
½ cup grated Parmesan cheese
1 teaspoon fennel seed
½ teaspoon dried oregano,
  crushed
1 8-ounce can pizza sauce
4 ounces sliced pepperoni
1 small green pepper, sliced
1 2½-ounce jar sliced
  mushrooms, drained

Cook lasagna noodles according to package directions; drain. In a skillet cook sausage till brown; drain off fat. Arrange *half* the cooked noodles in bottom of an ungreased 13x9x2-inch baking pan. Sprinkle ¾ *cup* of the mozzarella cheese, *half* of the Parmesan cheese, the fennel, and oregano over noodles. Top with remaining noodles. Spread pizza sauce over noodles. Arrange sausage, pepperoni, sliced green pepper, and sliced mushrooms atop. Bake, uncovered, in a 350° oven for 15 minutes. Sprinkle with remaining mozzarella and Parmesan cheese. Bake 15 minutes more or till hot. Cut into squares to serve. Makes 8 servings.

Dianne Scharton
Brighton, Colorado

SAUSAGE AND POTATO BAKE

When time is short, convenience products are an easy kitchen helper. This casserole makes good use of packaged au gratin potato mix--

2 5½-ounce packages dry au
  gratin potatoes
1 medium onion, sliced into
  thin wedges
4 cups boiling water
1¾ cups milk
1 10-ounce package frozen
  peas, thawed
1 1-pound Kielbasa sausage
  ring

In a 3-quart casserole combine the dry au gratin potatoes and sauce mix from the potatoes packages and the sliced onion. Stir in water and milk. Bake, covered, in a 350° oven for 45 minutes. Uncover. Stir in thawed peas. Make slashes in sausage about ½ inch deep and 1 inch apart. Place sausage atop potatoes. Continue baking, uncovered, about 30 minutes more or till potatoes are tender. Makes 6 servings.

Linda Siar
Hubbard, Ohio

44

BEEF ROAST AND NOODLES

1 3- to 3½-pound beef chuck
    pot roast
2 tablespoons all-purpose flour
2 teaspoons instant beef
    bouillon granules
  Dash garlic powder
2 bay leaves
2 large onions, sliced (2 cups)
½ cup catsup
⅓ cup packed brown sugar
¼ cup lemon juice
½ cup raisins
  Hot cooked noodles

Trim excess fat from meat; reserve
trimmings. Coat meat with flour. In
a 4½-quart Dutch oven heat trimmings till about *2 tablespoons* of fat
accumulate; discard trimmings.
Brown meat on both sides in hot
fat. Add bouillon granules and 1¼
cups *hot water*. Sprinkle with garlic
powder. Add bay leaves. Place onions atop and around meat. Cover;
bake in a 325° oven for 1½ hours.
Remove bay leaves; discard. Stir together catsup, brown sugar, and
lemon juice; pour over meat. Sprinkle with raisins. Cover; continue
baking 30 to 45 minutes more or
till meat is tender. Serve with hot
cooked noodles. Serves 8 to 10.

Carol Ann Bird

Carol Bird
Bensenville, Illinois

*This sauerbraten-like recipe makes
its own rich and tangy gravy. Serve
slices of the tender roast beef with
hot cooked noodles and ladle on the
raisin-studded sauce.*

United States

PEACHY MEAT LOAF PIE

Americans share a great appetite for ground beef, and meat loaves are one reflection of that taste. This lightly sweet and tangy version is pie shaped and served in wedges--

  1 8-ounce can sliced peaches
  1 slightly beaten egg
 ¼ cup catsup
  1 cup soft bread crumbs
1½ teaspoons minced dried
     onion
1½ teaspoons Worcestershire
     sauce
 ¾ teaspoon salt
 ¾ teaspoon dry mustard
1½ pounds lean ground beef
  2 tablespoons brown sugar
  1 tablespoon vinegar
  1 tablespoon catsup
 ½ teaspoon ground ginger

Drain peaches, reserving ¼ *cup* of the liquid. Set peaches aside. Combine egg, the ¼ cup peach liquid, and the ¼ cup catsup. Stir in bread crumbs, onion, Worcestershire sauce, salt, and dry mustard. Add ground beef; mix well. Pat the seasoned meat mixture evenly into bottom of a 9-inch pie plate without forming edges. Set pie plate on a pizza plate or baking sheet.

Bake in a 350° oven for 40 minutes or till done; spoon off fat, if necessary. Arrange peach slices in spoke-fashion over meat. Stir together brown sugar, vinegar, the 1 tablespoon catsup, and ginger. Carefully spoon over peaches and meat. Bake 10 minutes more. Remove to serving platter to serve. Cut into wedges. Makes 6 servings.

Mary Doumani
Mary Doumani
Andover, Massachusetts

OVEN-STYLE PORK RIBS

  4 pounds pork spareribs, cut
     into 2-rib portions
 ½ cup packed brown sugar
  2 teaspoons cornstarch
  2 teaspoons curry powder
 ½ teaspoon salt
 ¼ teaspoon ground ginger
  1 cup unsweetened
     grapefruit juice

Place pork ribs, meaty side down, in a shallow roasting pan. Roast ribs in a 450° oven for 30 minutes. Remove meat from oven; drain off excess fat. Turn ribs, meaty side up. Reduce oven temperature to 350°. Roast 30 minutes more.

Meanwhile, prepare fruit glaze. In a 1-quart saucepan combine brown sugar, cornstarch, curry powder, salt, and ginger; stir in grapefruit juice. Cook and stir over medium heat till mixture is thickened and bubbly. Cook and stir 2 minutes more. Spoon some of the fruit glaze over the ribs. Roast 25 minutes more or till meat is tender and thoroughly cooked, spooning some more of the fruit glaze over ribs occasionally. Brush with remaining glaze before serving. Makes 6 servings.

Donna Etzold
Donna Etzold
Perryville, Missouri

Red Raspberry Cream Cheese Pie capitalizes on the fresh flavor of ruby-red raspberries. Generously covered with succulent raspberries, this luscious dessert features mounds of fluffy cream cheese and whipping cream atop a golden, flaky piecrust. *(See recipe, page 48.)*

United States

RED RASPBERRY CREAM CHEESE PIE

Pictured on page 47--

    2 3-ounce packages cream
       cheese, softened
    ⅔ cup whipping cream
    1 9-inch baked pastry shell,
       cooled
    1 quart fresh red raspberries
    1 cup sugar
    ½ cup unsweetened pineapple
       juice
    ¼ cup cornstarch
       Unsweetened whipped
       cream

In medium bowl beat together softened cream cheese and the whipping cream. Spread mixture over
bottom of the cooled pie shell; chill.
   Reserve *half* of the raspberries.
In a large mixing bowl mash the remaining raspberries. Stir in sugar;
let stand about 1 hour. Sieve berry
mixture. In a saucepan combine
pineapple juice and cornstarch; stir
in sieved berry mixture. Cook and
stir over medium heat till berry
mixture is thickened and bubbly.
Reduce heat; cook and stir 2 minutes more. Remove from heat; let
cool. Spread *three-fourths* of the thickened berry mixture over cream
cheese layer in pie shell. Arrange
1½ cups of the reserved whole raspberries over top of pie. Spoon the
remaining cooked berry mixture
over whole berries. Chill about 2
hours or till set. Garnish with
whipped cream and reserved fresh
raspberries. Makes 8 servings.

Judy Snider
Brandon, South Dakota

FREEZER PEANUT BUTTER PIE

*There's more to peanut butter than jelly sand-
wiches. You can count on that creamy, nutty
taste in this rich frozen pie, too--*

    18 graham cracker squares
    ¼ cup granulated sugar
    6 tablespoons butter or
       margarine, melted
    1 8-ounce package cream
       cheese, softened
    ½ cup peanut butter
    1 cup sifted powdered sugar
    ½ cup milk
    1 8-ounce container frozen
       whipped dessert topping,
       thawed
    ¼ cup chopped peanuts

Place graham crackers in a plastic
bag or between 2 sheets of plastic
wrap or waxed paper. Crush into
fine crumbs; measure *1¼ cups*
crumbs. In mixing bowl combine
the crumbs and granulated sugar.
Stir in butter; toss to thoroughly
combine. Press crumb mixture onto
bottom and sides of a 9-inch pie
plate to form a firm, even crust.
Chill crust while making filling.
   In a large mixer bowl beat together softened cream cheese and
the peanut butter till well blended.
Beat in powdered sugar and milk.
Fold in thawed whipped dessert topping. Turn peanut butter mixture
into chilled graham cracker crust.
Sprinkle chopped peanuts atop.
Press peanuts gently into pie. Cover
and freeze 8 hours or overnight. Let
stand at room temperature 10 to 15
minutes before serving. Serves 8.

Cora Tenaglia
Brighton, Massachusetts

PEANUT BUTTER CHOCOLATE CHIP COOKIES

Chocolate chips are an integral part of American dessert baking. The original version was created in 1940 at the Toll House Inn in Massachusetts; hence the Toll House chocolate chip cookie. The added peanut butter in the dough makes this cookie extra special--

1¼ cups all-purpose flour
  2 teaspoons baking powder
¼ teaspoon salt
½ cup shortening
½ cup peanut butter
½ cup packed brown sugar
½ cup granulated sugar
  1 egg
½ teaspoon vanilla
  1 6-ounce package (1 cup) semisweet chocolate pieces

In a small mixing bowl stir together flour, baking powder, and salt; set aside. In a large mixer bowl beat together shortening and peanut butter for 30 seconds. Add the brown sugar and granulated sugar, beating till mixture is light and fluffy. Add egg and vanilla; beat well. Stir flour mixture into beaten mixture. Stir in the chocolate pieces. Roll dough into 1-inch balls and place 2 inches apart on an ungreased cookie sheet. Bake cookies in a 375° oven about 10 minutes or till golden. Cool on wire rack. Makes about 4 dozen.

Cecilia Piner
Cecilia Piner
Cedar Creek, Nebraska

BEST CHOCOLATE BROWNIES

Since the 1920s, Americans have had a liking for brownies. Whether chewy and fudgy or cake-like in texture, these bars still make a favorite chocolate treat--

1 cup butter or margarine
4 squares (4 ounces) unsweetened chocolate
2 cups sugar
4 eggs
1 cup all-purpose flour
1 teaspoon baking powder
2 teaspoons vanilla
1 cup chopped walnuts
1 6-ounce package (1 cup) semisweet chocolate pieces

In a 2-quart saucepan melt butter or margarine and unsweetened chocolate squares over low heat. Transfer chocolate mixture to a large mixer bowl. Add sugar; mix well. Add eggs, one at a time, beating just till blended. In a mixing bowl stir together flour and baking powder. Add to chocolate mixture along with the vanilla; mix well.

Pour batter into a greased and floured 13x9x2-inch baking pan. Sprinkle with the chopped walnuts and chocolate pieces. Bake in a 325° oven about 45 minutes or till done. Cool on a wire rack. Cut into bars. Makes 32 bars.

Laura Daniel
Laura Daniel
Huntley, Illinois

United States

APPLE HARVEST CAKE

1¼ cups all-purpose flour
1 cup whole wheat flour
1 cup granulated sugar
¾ cup packed brown sugar
1 tablespoon ground cinnamon
2 teaspoons baking powder
1 teaspoon salt
½ teaspoon baking soda
¾ cup cooking oil
1 teaspoon vanilla
3 eggs
2 cups finely chopped, peeled
   apples (2 medium)
1 cup chopped walnuts
   Powdered Sugar Glaze
   (recipe below)
   or whipped cream

Generously grease and flour a 10-inch fluted tube pan; set aside. In a large mixing bowl combine the flours, granulated and brown sugars, cinnamon, baking powder, salt, and baking soda. Add oil, vanilla, and the eggs; beat till well mixed. Stir in chopped apples and walnuts. Spoon batter evenly into prepared pan. Bake in a 350° oven for 45 to 50 minutes or till cake tests done. Cool in pan 15 minutes; invert cake onto a wire rack. Cool thoroughly. Drizzle top with Powdered Sugar Glaze or dollop servings with sweetened whipped cream. Makes 16 servings.

Powdered Sugar Glaze: In a small mixing bowl stir together ½ cup sifted *powdered sugar,* ¼ teaspoon *vanilla,* and enough *milk* (1 to 2 teaspoons) to make of drizzling consistency. Drizzle over cooled cake.

Susan Adams
Susan Adams
Barre, Vermont

SOUR CREAM PECAN POUND CAKE

Pound cakes were originally made with a pound each of butter, sugar, eggs, and flour--

1 cup butter or margarine
2¾ cups sugar
6 egg yolks
1 teaspoon vanilla
½ teaspoon lemon extract
½ teaspoon almond extract
   (optional)
3 cups all-purpose flour
¼ teaspoon baking soda
1 8-ounce carton (1 cup)
   dairy sour cream
1 cup chopped pecans
6 egg whites

Grease and flour a 10-inch tube pan; set aside. In a large mixer bowl thoroughly cream butter or margarine and *2¼ cups* of the sugar till light. Add egg yolks, one at a time, beating well after each addition. Add vanilla and the lemon and almond extracts; beat till light. Stir together flour and baking soda. Add flour mixture alternately with sour cream to beaten egg yolk mixture, beginning and ending with flour mixture. Stir in chopped pecans. Wash beaters thoroughly. In a large mixing bowl beat egg whites till soft peaks form. Gradually beat in the remaining ½ cup sugar. Fold beaten egg whites into cake batter. Turn batter into prepared tube pan. Bake in a 325° oven about 80 minutes or till cake tests done. Cool cake in pan 10 minutes; remove from pan and cool completely on wire rack. Makes 16 servings.

Linda Traylor
Linda Traylor
Chattanooga, Tennessee

BANANA SPLIT DESSERT

- 2 cups graham cracker crumbs
- ½ cup butter, melted
- ½ cup butter or margarine
- 2 cups sifted powdered sugar
- 2 eggs
- 5 bananas
- 1 15½-ounce can crushed pineapple, well drained
- 1 8-ounce container frozen whipped dessert topping, thawed

    Semisweet chocolate, shredded
- ⅓ cup chopped nuts (optional)

    Maraschino cherries

In a mixing bowl toss together the graham cracker crumbs and the melted ½ cup butter. Press crumb mixture onto bottom of a 13x9x2-inch baking pan. In a small mixer bowl beat the remaining ½ cup butter about 30 seconds till softened. Add powdered sugar; beat till fluffy. Beat in eggs. Spread egg mixture over crumb mixture. Slice bananas lengthwise into halves and arrange over egg mixture. Spoon pineapple over bananas. Spread with dessert topping. Sprinkle with chocolate and the nuts, if desired. Cover; refrigerate at least 4 hours before serving. Cut into squares to serve. Top each with a cherry. Cover and chill to store. Serves 15.

Beverly Hiler

Beverly Hiler
Fremont, Michigan

Get all the great flavors of a banana split in a convenient refrigerator dessert. Banana Split Dessert boasts layers of creamy filling, bananas, pineapple, and whipped topping.

Puerto Rico

In Puerto Rico, and neighboring Caribbean islands, dozens of tasty recipes are launched from a similar herb base. Known as "sofrito," this aromatic and well-seasoned sauce is a combination of green peppers, onions, garlic, tomatoes, coriander, and annatto seed (sometimes called achiote).

Chicken, rice, and beans represent the food staples of Puerto Rico. Although recipes vary slightly from house to house, few dishes are minus the sofrito. Red Beans and Rice is perhaps the most popular of Puerto Rican foods. Enjoyed for its rich and distinctive flavor, sofrito is credited for much of its zesty taste. Featured on this page is Puerto Rican Fried Chicken. Tender pieces of chicken are simmered in sofrito, then coated in crumbs and fried till crisp and golden. The sofrito sauce is thickened slightly and served with the chicken.

RICE-GARBANZO BAKE

1⅔ cups long grain rice
1 15-ounce can garbanzo beans
1 10¾-ounce can condensed chicken broth
8 ounces cubed cooked beef, chicken, or ham (1½ cups)
1 cup water
1 large onion, chopped (1 cup)
1 3-ounce can sliced mushrooms
¼ cup snipped parsley
¼ teaspoon pepper
6 slices bacon, crisp cooked, drained, and crumbled
1 cup shredded cheddar cheese (4 ounces)

In a 2-quart casserole combine *uncooked* rice, *undrained* garbanzo beans, chicken broth, choice of cubed meat, water, onion, *undrained* mushrooms, parsley, and pepper.

Cover and bake in a 350° oven for 60 minutes or till rice is tender, stirring once. Stir again, then sprinkle with the crumbled bacon and shredded cheddar cheese. Bake, uncovered, for 4 to 5 minutes more or till the cheese is melted. Makes 8 servings.

Luz S. Cintron

Luz S. Cintron
Toa Baja, Puerto Rico

FRIED CHICKEN

3 pounds chicken thighs and drumsticks
Sofrito (recipe below)
2 tablespoons all-purpose flour
2 tablespoons cornstarch
2 tablespoons fine dry bread crumbs
Cooking oil for frying
1 5⅓-ounce can (⅔ cup) evaporated milk
4 teaspoons all-purpose flour

Place chicken in a large skillet. Combine ½ cup *water* and Sofrito; pour over chicken. Cook, covered, about 30 minutes or till chicken is tender, turning once. Stir together the 2 tablespoons flour, the cornstarch, bread crumbs, ½ teaspoon *salt*, and ⅛ teaspoon *pepper*. Remove chicken pieces from sofrito mixture; dip in flour mixture to coat.

In another large skillet heat ½-inch oil till very hot. Fry chicken pieces in hot oil till browned, about 45 seconds per side, turning once. Drain; keep warm. Skim fat from sofrito mixture. Blend together milk and the 4 teaspoons flour. Stir into sofrito mixture. Cook and stir till bubbly; cook and stir 1 minute more. Serve with chicken. Serves 6.

Sofrito: In a small skillet combine 2 slices *bacon*, chopped; ¼ cup chopped, peeled *tomato*; ¼ cup chopped *onion*; 2 tablespoons chopped *green pepper*; 1 large clove *garlic*, minced; ¼ teaspoon *salt*; and ½ teaspoon *paprika*. Cook, covered, 6 to 7 minutes or till vegetables are tender. Stir in 1 teaspoon *lime juice*.

Ivonne Jimenez

Ivonne Jimenez
Guaynabo, Puerto Rico

SWEET POTATO-PUMPKIN PUDDINGS

1 8-ounce can sweet potatoes
    (vacuum packed), drained
1 cup canned pumpkin
½ teaspoon finely shredded
    orange peel
⅓ cup sugar
2 tablespoons all-purpose flour
1 teaspoon ground cinnamon
¼ teaspoon ground cloves
2 beaten eggs
1 cup canned unsweetened
    coconut milk
   Sweetened whipped cream
   Toasted shredded coconut
    (optional)

Mash sweet potatoes in food processor or put through a sieve. In a large mixing bowl combine pumpkin, mashed sweet potatoes, and orange peel. In another mixing bowl stir together sugar, flour, cinnamon, cloves, and ¼ teaspoon *salt;* stir into pumpkin mixture. Add beaten eggs and coconut milk; mix well. Spoon mixture evenly into six 6-ounce soufflé cups or custard cups.

   Bake in 350° oven about 50 minutes or set in center. Serve with dollops of whipped cream. Garnish with coconut, if desired. Serves 6.

Cidia Robles
Bayamon, Puerto Rico

*Puerto Ricans enjoy baked puddings
for a light but special ending to a
meal. Individual Sweet Potato-
Pumpkin Puddings are a creamy
medley of fluffy sweet potatoes and
pumpkin, subtly flavored with
orange peel and spices.*

WESTERN

EUROPE

England

Teatime in the British Isles became the institution it is today in the latter half of the 19th Century.

Tea is more than simply a drink to the English--it kicks off another work day, welcomes a mid-morning break in work at the office or factory, serves as a mealtime accompaniment, and relaxes the soul before bedtime.

But this age-old tradition is most popularly recognized when the clock chimes four and the English sit down to enjoy "cuppa", a cup of tea accompanied by assorted sweet treats and little sandwiches.

YORKSHIRE CURD TART

1 cup all-purpose flour
3 tablespoons sugar
¼ cup butter or margarine
1 egg yolk
2 tablespoons cold water
2 cups ricotta cheese or
    sieved cottage cheese
¾ cup sugar
2 tablespoons butter or
    margarine, melted
2 beaten eggs
½ teaspoon pumpkin pie spice
⅔ cup currants or raisins

For crust, in a mixing bowl stir together flour and the 3 tablespoons sugar; cut in the ¼ cup butter or margarine till crumbly. Beat egg yolk with water. Drizzle over flour mixture. Toss with fork to mix. On a lightly floured surface, roll pastry to a 12-inch circle; fit into a 9-inch pie plate. Trim and flute edges. Bake in a 400° oven for 10 minutes or till light brown.

Meanwhile, for filling, combine ricotta cheese or cottage cheese, the ¾ cup sugar, the 2 tablespoons melted butter or margarine, the beaten eggs, and pumpkin pie spice. Mix well. Stir in currants. Pour into prepared crust. Cover edge of pie with foil; bake in 375° oven for 20 minutes. Remove foil. Continue baking for 15 to 20 minutes more or till filling is set. Cool. Makes 6 to 8 servings.

N. Buckingham
Tunbridge Wells, England

RABBIT-CIDER CASSEROLE

⅓ cup butter or margarine
1 2- to 2½ pound rabbit,
    cut up, or one 2½- to
    3-pound broiler-fryer
    chicken, cut up
1¼ cups chopped onion
1 cup chopped carrots
⅓ cup broken walnuts
2 2½-ounce jars whole
    mushrooms, drained
2 tablespoons all-purpose flour
1 teaspoon salt
¼ teaspoon pepper
1 cup apple juice or cider

In a large skillet melt butter or margarine; cook rabbit or chicken pieces till browned on all sides. Transfer meat to a 3-quart casserole, reserving drippings in skillet. Add the onion, carrot, and walnuts to drippings; cook till vegetables are tender but not brown. Stir in mushrooms. Spoon vegetables and nuts over meat in casserole, reserving drippings in skillet. Blend flour, salt, and pepper into drippings. Add apple juice all at once. Cook and stir till thickened and bubbly. Cook and stir 1 minute more. Pour over meat and vegetables. Bake, covered, in a 350° oven for 1 hour or till meat is done. Serves 4 to 6.

E. Brown
Taunton, England

cotland

Tea scones, or "sgonnes" by their Gaelic name, are a favorite of immigrants from all over the British Isles. The Scots take credit for them, but immigrants of British and Welsh extraction claim them, too.

Country housewives fondly refer to these griddle cakes as "singing hinnies" because of the way they would sing and fizz when originally cooked over an open fire. Today, many cooks drop or shape scones on baking sheets and bake, or pat the dough into an oven-going skillet, bake, and serve cut into wedges.

These famous biscuits are usually spread with butter or jam, and for special occasions, are served with fresh strawberries and cream. Scones may also contain dried fruit, currants or raisins, chopped apple, cheese, maple syrup, or molasses.

TREACLE TEA SCONES

Treacle, or Scotch molasses, is sweeter and thicker than the molasses in the United States. Substitute American molasses for Scotch treacle if you can't find it in specialty stores--

- 2 cups all-purpose flour
- 1 tablespoon sugar
- 1 teaspoon baking soda
- 1 teaspoon cream of tartar
- ½ teaspoon ground allspice
- ¼ teaspoon salt
- 6 tablespoons butter or margarine
- ¾ cup milk
- 2 tablespoons treacle or molasses

In a mixing bowl stir together flour, sugar, soda, cream of tartar, allspice, and salt. Cut in the butter or margarine till mixture resembles coarse crumbs. Make a well in center; stir in milk and treacle or molasses just till moistened. Spread in lightly greased 10-inch oven-going skillet. Cook, covered, over medium-low heat for 20 to 25 minutes or till golden on bottom and set on edges. Place skillet under broiler 4 inches from heat; broil for 4 to 5 minutes till golden. Serve scones spread with butter and jam. Makes 12 servings.

COCK-A-LEEKIE SOUP

The Scots have proclaimed this hearty chicken-and-leek soup as their national soup--

- 1 2½- to 3-pound broiler-fryer chicken, cut up
- 4 cups water
- ½ cup finely chopped carrot
- ½ cup finely chopped celery
- ¼ cup finely chopped onion
- 2 sprigs parsley
- 2 teaspoons salt
- ¼ teaspoon white pepper
- 1 bay leaf
- 2 medium leeks, thinly sliced (1½ cups)
- 1 small potato, peeled and diced (½ cup)
- ½ cup quick-cooking barley
- ½ cup pitted, dried prunes, snipped
- 2 cups light cream or milk
  Sliced leeks (optional)

Rinse chicken pieces. In a large saucepan or Dutch oven combine chicken pieces, water, carrot, celery, onion, parsley, salt, white pepper, and bay leaf. Bring to boiling; reduce heat. Cover and simmer about 25 minutes or till chicken is tender. Remove chicken pieces from broth. Skim off fat. Remove bay leaf and parsley. When chicken is cool enough to handle, remove and discard skin and bones. Cut up chicken. Add chicken, leeks, potato, barley, and prunes to broth. Bring to boiling; reduce heat. Cover and simmer for 15 to 20 minutes or till potato is tender. Stir in cream or milk. Heat through. Garnish each serving with additional sliced leeks, if desired. Makes 6 to 8 servings.

Wales

Classic Welsh Rabbit is simply toasted thick slices of bread, spread with spicy mustard, topped with a slab of robust cheese, and toasted under the broiler. One account credits a Welshman with creating and naming this rib-sticking dish when he ran out of meat and was forced to serve cheese and bread to guests.

Today versions of this economical mainstay, sometimes referred to as Welsh Rarebit, include a cheddar cheese mixture spooned over toast points. Some cooks use a combination of cheeses in the sauce, or stir in bits of meat or vegetables for a more substantial dish. Frequently, a liquid such as milk, beer, or wine is used to thin the golden cheese sauce.

LAMB WITH HONEY

1 5½- to 6-pound leg of lamb
1 teaspoon ground ginger
½ teaspoon dried rosemary, crushed
1 cup apple cider or juice
⅔ cup honey
1 tablespoon cornstarch
6 medium potatoes, peeled and thinly sliced
5 tablespoons butter
2 medium onions, thinly sliced

Line a shallow roasting pan with foil. Rub meat with mixture of ginger, 1 teaspoon *salt,* and ¼ teaspoon *pepper.* Place, fat side up, in roasting pan. Sprinkle with rosemary. Combine cider and honey; set aside. Bake lamb, uncovered, in a 325° oven for 1 hour. Pour honey mixture over meat; bake 1½ hours more or till meat thermometer registers 160°, basting occasionally with pan juices. Remove meat to platter; keep warm. Drain fat from pan drippings. Measure *1 cup* pan juices. In saucepan blend cornstarch with 1 tablespoon *water;* add the 1 cup pan juices. Cook and stir till thickened; cook and stir 2 minutes more. Serve with Onion Cake. Serves 6.

Onion Cake: In a well greased 2-quart casserole place *one-third* of the potatoes; sprinkle with *salt* and *pepper* and dot with *1 tablespoon* of the butter. Top with *half* the onions; dot with *1 tablespoon* more butter. Repeat layers, ending with potatoes and the remaining butter. Bake, covered, in a 325° oven for 1 hour. Uncover; bake 30 minutes more.

Lorraine Clotter

L. Norton
Cardiff, Wales

BARA BRITH BREAD

"Bara brith" in Welsh means speckled bread--

2¼ to 2¾ cups all-purpose flour
1 package active dry yeast
¼ teaspoon ground cinnamon
⅛ teaspoon ground nutmeg
⅛ teaspoon ground cloves
⅔ cup buttermilk
¼ cup packed brown sugar
¼ cup butter or margarine
1 egg
⅔ cup dried currants or raisins

Combine *1¼ cups* of the flour, yeast, cinnamon, nutmeg, and cloves. In saucepan heat buttermilk, brown sugar, butter, and ½ teaspoon *salt* just till warm (115° to 120°) and butter is almost melted; stir constantly. Add to flour mixture; add egg. Beat at low speed of electric mixer ½ minute. Beat 3 minutes at high speed. Stir in currants and as much of the remaining flour as you can mix in with a spoon. Turn out onto floured surface. Knead in enough remaining flour to make a moderately stiff dough that is smooth and elastic (6 to 8 minutes total). Shape into a ball. Place in greased bowl; turn once. Cover; let rise till double (about 1¼ hours). Punch down. Shape into a loaf; place in greased 8x4x2-inch loaf pan. Cover; let rise till nearly double (about 30 minutes). Bake in a 375° oven 35 to 40 minutes; cover with foil last 20 minutes. Remove from pan; cool. Makes 1 loaf.

Tender, juicy lamb is a tradition in Wales. Baste Lamb with Honey with the golden rosemary-honey glaze. Then, accompany slices of meat with Onion Cake or with brussels sprouts, leeks, and potatoes.

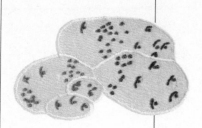

Ireland

The versatility of potatoes is evident in the British Isles. Irish "colcannon" is a mixture of mashed potatoes and cabbage, moistened with lots of butter and cream. There are also thick and creamy potato soup, tender potato-apple cake, and "boxty" (potato pancakes). Likewise, the Scots dote on their mashed potatoes called "chappit tatties", and the English love "stovies", buttery potatoes boiled for a long time on the stove.

Historically, potatoes came to Ireland from the New World in the 17th Century, and have been a mainstay of the Irish diet ever since. In the cool, moist climate and fertile soil of Ireland, potatoes thrived and were quickly recognized as a nutritious "filler" food. Everyone planted them and depended on them as their economical dietary staple. At one time, potatoes even threatened to replace bread!

GAELIC CHOPS

The Irish are often credited with the invention of whiskey, although the rivalry between Irish and Scottish distillers still persists. Here it is the subtle flavor in the cream sauce spooned over tender lamb chops--

    4 lamb leg shoulder chops, cut
        ½ inch thick
    1 tablespoon butter or
        margarine
      Salt and freshly ground
        black pepper
    ¼ cup whipping cream
    1 tablespoon Irish whiskey
      Watercress or snipped
        parsley (optional)

Trim excess fat from chops. In a 10-inch skillet brown chops in hot butter or margarine on both sides. Sprinkle chops lightly with some salt and pepper. Reduce heat. Cover and simmer for 15 minutes, adding a little more butter, if necessary. Remove chops to a heated serving platter; keep warm.

Spoon excess fat from pan juices. Stir in whipping cream and whiskey. Heat gently till hot, stirring up the brown bits in skillet; *do not boil.* Immediately pour the cream sauce over lamb chops. Garnish with watercress or snipped parsley, if desired. Makes 4 servings.

Patricia Conroy
Patricia Conroy
Rosenallis, Ireland

COLCANNON

    1 pound potatoes, peeled
        and cut up (3 medium)
    2 tablespoons milk
    ¼ teaspoon salt
    ⅛ teaspoon pepper
    ½ pound chopped kale or
        cabbage (2 cups)
    2 tablespoons butter or
        margarine
    ¼ cup chopped onion
      Butter or margarine

In a 2-quart saucepan cook potatoes in boiling salted water about 20 minutes or till tender; drain. Transfer potatoes to a mixer bowl; mash. Add the milk, salt, and pepper; beat at low speed of electric mixer till fluffy. In the same saucepan cook kale or cabbage in boiling water for 5 to 7 minutes or till tender; drain.

Meanwhile, in an 8-inch skillet melt the 2 tablespoons butter or margarine. Add chopped onion. Cook over low heat about 5 minutes or till onion is tender. Add the mashed potatoes and the cooked kale or cabbage. Heat through, stirring constantly. Pile the potato mixture into a heated serving dish. Score top with a fork. Serve hot with pats of butter or margarine atop. Makes 4 servings.

Jerry Hutchinson
Jerry Hutchinson
Portarlington, Ireland

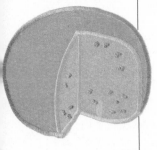

etherlands

The cool, damp Dutch climate makes hearty meals a must. Most families eat a big breakfast with eggs, cheese, and sliced meat along with bread and hot cereal. The main meal of the day is in the evening. In the winter this is often pea soup or hodgepodge, a one-dish meal made of potatoes, sausages, and cabbage. Fresh vegetables are plentiful all year round, grown in acres of greenhouses. Eel, from the canals, is served often, and herring is so popular that it's available from carts in the streets for a snack or quick lunch.

Many Dutch restaurants offer the rijsttafel (rice table), a tradition which came originally from the Indonesian colonies. The rice is served with as many as 25 dishes of seafood, eggs, vegetables, and meat.

GELDERLAND STEW

2½ cups dry red kidney beans
6 slices bacon
1 pound cubed boneless
   pork
3 medium onions, sliced
1 tablespoon prepared
   mustard
2 teaspoons beef bouillon
   granules
½ teaspoon nutmeg
1 1-pound can tomatoes,
   cut up
4 cups cubed peeled potato
1 cup sliced celery
1 cup green pepper strips
3 cups shredded cabbage

Rinse kidney beans. In Dutch oven combine beans and 8 cups *water.* Bring to boiling. Reduce heat; simmer 2 minutes. Remove from heat. Cover; let stand 1 hour. (Or, soak beans in water overnight.) Drain. Cook bacon till crisp; drain, reserving 3 tablespoons drippings. Crumble bacon; set aside. Brown pork cubes in reserved drippings; add pork to beans. Cook onion in remaining drippings till tender; add to beans along with mustard, bouillon granules, 2 teaspoons *salt,* nutmeg, and ¼ teaspoon *pepper.* Add 6 cups fresh *water.* Bring to boiling; reduce heat. Cover; simmer 50 minutes or till beans are nearly tender. Add *undrained* tomatoes, potatoes, and celery. Simmer, covered, 20 to 25 minutes. Add green pepper and cabbage; simmer, covered, 5 to 10 minutes or till vegetables are tender. Add bacon. Serves 10 to 12.

Ans Kohlen
Nymegen, Netherlands

FRUITED BUTTERMILK RING

2 envelopes unflavored gelatin
⅓ cup sugar
5½ cups buttermilk
1 teaspoon shredded
   lemon peel
¼ cup lemon juice
2 cups halved strawberries,
   raspberries, dark sweet
   cherries, nectarine or
   peach slices, or orange
   sections, or well-drained
   canned apricot halves,
   pineapple chunks, or
   peach slices, or a
   combination of fruits
1 beaten egg yolk
¼ cup sifted powdered sugar
¼ teaspoon vanilla
½ cup whipping cream

In saucepan stir together gelatin and sugar; add 2 cups of the buttermilk. Cook and stir over low heat till gelatin and sugar dissolve. Cool 15 minutes. Add remaining buttermilk, lemon peel, and lemon juice. Pour into 6-cup mold. Cover and chill overnight. Unmold onto serving plate. Arrange assorted fruit around mold. Spoon some of the Vanilla Sauce over; pass remaining sauce. Makes 12 servings.

Vanilla Sauce: In small mixing bowl combine egg yolk, powdered sugar, and vanilla. Beat till smooth and well combined. In small mixer bowl whip cream to soft peaks; fold in egg yolk mixture. Cover; chill. Stir before serving. Makes 1½ cups.

A. Mol Cnossen
Leeuwarden, Netherlands

Belgium

In northern Belgium, the language and food are similar to those of the nearby Netherlands; in the south most people speak French and cook like their French neighbors. But many foods are distinctively Belgian. Belgian endive and Brussels sprouts grow better here than anywhere else in the world. Waterzooi is a truly Belgian dish said to be the favorite supper of the king. It's a soup made with fish or chicken in an herbed broth which may be thickened with eggs and cream. Good cooks often season dishes with a pinch of chervil or nutmeg, and prefer shallots and leeks to onions. Belgian fast-food fans enjoy mussels with french fries and beer.

Sunday is family day here, when all the children gather at mother's house for a special dinner, or for a drive or walk followed by a fine restaurant meal.

OSTEND WATERZOOI

  1 pound fresh or frozen
     fish fillets
  1 pound fresh or frozen
     lobster tails
 20 mussels
  2 leeks, sliced
  2 stalks celery, sliced
  2 tablespoons butter or
     margarine
 1½ teaspoons dried marjoram,
     crushed
  4 teaspoons instant chicken
     bouillon granules
  1 tablespoon snipped parsley

Thaw fish, if frozen. Cut into 1-inch pieces. Partially thaw lobster; remove from shells. Split tails in half lengthwise; cut into 1-inch pieces. Wash mussels; cover with salted water using 1 gallon cold *water* and ⅓ cup *salt*. Let stand 15 minutes; rinse. Repeat soaking and rinsing twice. Cook leeks and celery in butter till tender. Stir in marjoram and ½ teaspoon *pepper*. Set aside. In Dutch oven combine mussels and 4 cups *water*. Bring to boiling; reduce heat. Cover; simmer 5 minutes or till mussels open. Remove with slotted spoon. Remove mussels from shells; set aside. Return water to boiling. Add fish and lobster. Simmer 4 to 5 minutes, covered, till fish flakes easily when tested. Remove with slotted spoon. Strain cooking liquid and return to Dutch oven. Add mussels to liquid with fish, lobster, leek-celery mixture, and bouillon granules. Heat through. Sprinkle with parsley. Makes 6 servings

Mireille Cardyn
Ostend, Belgium

GLAZED ONIONS

 ¼ cup sugar
  3 tablespoons water
  3 tablespoons butter or
     margarine
  1 tablespoon white
     wine vinegar
  1 tablespoon tomato paste
 ½ teaspoon salt
 ½ teaspoon dried thyme,
     crushed
 ⅛ teaspoon pepper
  1 bay leaf
  2 16-ounce packages frozen
     small white onions
 ¾ cup raisins

In 10-inch skillet combine sugar, water, butter or margarine, wine vinegar, tomato paste, salt, thyme, pepper, and bay leaf. Bring to boiling, stirring to dissolve sugar. Add onions and raisins. Return to boiling. Cover; reduce heat and simmer 10 minutes. Uncover and cook 20 to 25 minutes more over medium heat, stirring frequently till glazed. Remove bay leaf. Serve warm with pork or veal. Makes 6 to 8 servings.

Simone Debeys-Van Geert
Brussels, Belgium

STUFFED BACON ROLLS

12 slices bacon
 1 medium onion, chopped
 2 cloves garlic, minced
 1 egg
½ cup tomato sauce
¾ cup soft bread crumbs
      (1 slice)
 1 4-ounce can sliced
      mushrooms, drained
 2 tablespoons snipped parsley
 1 pound ground beef

Partially cook bacon. Drain; reserve
2 tablespoons drippings. Set bacon
aside. Cook onion and garlic in reserved drippings till tender but not
brown. In bowl combine egg and
tomato sauce; stir in bread crumbs,
mushrooms, onion mixture, parsley,
¼ teaspoon *salt*, and ⅛ teaspoon *pepper*. Add meat; mix well. Divide
into 4 parts. Place 2 slices bacon
side by side on waxed paper. Cut
another slice in half crosswise. Place
the 2 half-slices at one end of bacon
slices, overlapping slightly. Pat ¼ of
meat mixture evenly over bacon;
roll up jelly-roll style, starting from
narrow end. Place rolls seam side
down on rack in 12x7½x2-inch baking dish. Repeat with remaining bacon and meat. Bake in 350° oven
for about 40 minutes for medium
doneness. Makes 4 servings.

*Louise Nesslany
Ghent, Belgium*

*Plump, juicy Stuffed Bacon Rolls
are filled with a savory ground beef
and mushroom mixture. Serve with
buttered carrots or brussels sprouts.*

Sweden

The Swedish word smorgasbord means "bread and butter table," but the smorgasbord table of a Swedish restaurant holds dozens of other dishes. The century-old tradition has four parts: herring, the cold fish selection, cold meats and salads, and hot dishes. Each part consists of several choices and each is eaten separately from a clean plate. Don't bother to count your trips to the table--no one keeps track!

The legendary Viking past lives on in Sweden in such foods as oysters, cheese, cabbage, apples, onions, berries, and wild game. Reindeer meat is still eaten today. The reindeer venison and beef are often chopped or used in sausage in order to stretch these expensive meats and to make them more tender. Dill flavors many meat and fish dishes.

SAUCY HAM ROLL-UPS

Velvety rich sauce tops onion-and-mushroom-filled ham rolls for an easy, elegant company-best main dish--

2 tablespoons dry sherry
8 slices boiled ham
1 medium onion, chopped
1 tablespoon butter or
    margarine
1 3-ounce can sliced
    mushrooms, drained
½ cup whipping cream
2 tablespoons tomato paste
2 teaspoons all-purpose flour
½ teaspoon curry powder
½ cup shredded cheddar cheese
Hot cooked rice

Pour sherry over ham slices in a 10x6x2-inch baking dish. Marinate in refrigerator 2 hours, turning slices several times. In small skillet cook onion in butter or margarine till tender; add mushrooms. Spoon about 1 tablespoon of the onion mixture along one short side of each ham slice. Roll up the ham slices, starting at filled side, and place seam side down in the sherry in the 10x6x2-inch baking dish. Using wire whip combine whipping cream, tomato paste, flour, and curry powder; mix well. Pour over ham. Bake, covered, in 350° oven for 20 minutes. Sprinkle shredded cheese atop. Bake, uncovered, 5 minutes longer. Serve with hot cooked rice. Makes 4 servings.

Gunvi Soderlund

Gunvi Soderlund
Malmo, Sweden

LINGONBERRY ICE CREAM

Lingonberries, tiny and tart, are one of the most beloved of all Swedish foods. Look for the canned sauce in the gourmet sections of department or grocery stores--

3 beaten egg yolks
⅓ cup sugar
⅓ cup water
1 cup whipping cream,
    whipped
1 cup lingonberry sauce or
    cranberry-orange relish
Whipped cream (optional)
Grated chocolate (optional)

In small saucepan combine egg yolks, sugar, and water. Cook over low heat, stirring constantly, till thickened. Cool. Fold into whipped cream. Fold in lingonberry sauce or cranberry orange relish. Turn into 9x5x3-inch loaf pan. Freeze 8 hours or till firm. Remove from freezer 10 minutes before serving. Top each serving with whipped cream and grated chocolate, if desired.

Anita Borbos

Anita Borbos
Loeddekoepinge, Sweden

HERRING IN CREAM SAUCE

8 to 12 ounces pickled cut
    herring or pickled herring
    fillets
¼ cup mayonnaise or salad
    dressing
2 tablespoons whipping cream
¼ teaspoon sugar
⅛ teaspoon lemon pepper
⅛ teaspoon Worcestershire
    sauce
½ cup chopped red onion
½ cup sliced leek
    Fresh dillweed
    Coarsely ground pepper
1 tablespoon red caviar

Drain herring, reserving *1 tablespoon*
of the marinade. Combine mayonnaise or salad dressing, whipping
cream, sugar, lemon pepper,
Worcestershire sauce, and the reserved marinade. Reserve some of
the dillweed for garnish. Arrange
half the onion, half the leeks, and
half of the remaining dill on a serving plate. Sprinkle with pepper. Arrange herring atop. Top with
remaining onion, sliced leeks, and
dill. Spread with mayonnaise mixture. Garnish with reserved dill and
caviar. Makes 8 appetizer servings.

Maj-Lis Bodin
Maj-Lis Bodin
Tidaholm, Sweden

*Herring prepared in many ways
makes up the first course of the
traditional Swedish smorgasbord.
Herring in Cream Sauce is an
appetizer as refreshing as a cool
north breeze.*

France

French cooking is world famous, but most people think first of the elaborate classic cuisine prepared by professional chefs. Provincial cooking is home cooking, done by women all over the country using the finest local ingredients. Bread and most produce and meats are purchased fresh each day.

French families eat their main meal at noon and many offices and schools close for two hours to allow for leisurely dining. This noon dinner begins with an hors d'oeuvre course, followed by fish, meat, or fowl. Papa chooses an appropriate wine to accompany the entrée. Vegetables or a mixed green salad may be served with the main course or after it. Cheese and fruit usually complete the meal. On a special occasion, a rich dessert may be served. Demitasse, small cups of strong coffee, come after dessert, never with it.

STRAWBERRIES AND CREAM CAKE

4 egg yolks
⅔ cup sugar
⅓ cup water
4 teaspoons lemon juice
1 cup all-purpose flour
1 teaspoon baking powder
⅓ cup sugar
4 egg whites
1 cup whipping cream
1 cup Crème Fraîche (recipe page 69)
2 tablespoons sugar
1 teaspoon vanilla
2 to 3 tablespoons Kirsch
4 cups halved strawberries

In small mixer bowl beat egg yolks and ⅔ cup sugar for 10 minutes or till thick. Add water and lemon juice. Stir together flour and baking powder; stir into egg mixture. Wash mixer beaters. In large mixer bowl beat egg whites with ⅓ cup sugar till stiff; fold into batter. Turn into ungreased 10-inch tube pan. Bake in 325° oven about 50 minutes. Invert; cool completely. Loosen from pan; remove.

Combine whipping cream, Crème Fraîche, and the 2 tablespoons sugar; beat till very soft peaks form, being careful not to overbeat. Fold in vanilla. Cut cake into three layers; sprinkle each layer with a little Kirsch. Place the top layer, cut surface up, on serving plate. Top with ⅓ of the strawberries and ⅓ of the whipped cream mixture. Repeat twice. Chill about 2 hours. Makes 12 servings.

Maryse Antil
Bosc-le-Hard, France

CHEESE PUFF

This delectable breakfast or brunch dish is like a giant cheesey popover--

1 cup milk
½ cup butter or margarine
½ teaspoon salt
¼ teaspoon nutmeg
Dash pepper
1 cup all-purpose flour
4 eggs
1½ cups shredded Gruyère or Swiss cheese (6 ounces)

Generously grease an 8-inch round baking dish with butter. In medium saucepan combine milk, butter, salt, nutmeg, and pepper; bring to boiling. Add flour all at once; cook and stir vigorously till mixture forms a ball that doesn't separate. Remove from heat. Cool 5 minutes. Add eggs, one at a time, beating vigorously by hand after each addition till smooth. Stir *1¼ cups* of the shredded cheese into the egg mixture. Turn dough into prepared baking dish. Sprinkle with remaining cheese. Bake in 400° oven for 40 to 45 minutes. Makes 6 servings.

Marcelle Ofleidi
Marseille, France

A French version of strawberry shortcake, Strawberries and Cream Cake, is luscious in looks and taste. The fluffy filling is made with crème fraîche, a smooth, tangy cultured cream product you can prepare in your own kitchen.

France

VEAL BIRDS

1 pound veal leg round steak
4 thin slices ham
4 hard-cooked eggs
2 tablespoons all-purpose flour
2 tablespoons butter or
    margarine
1 teaspoon beef bouillon
    granules
1 cup sliced mushrooms
2 tablespoons sliced green
    onion
    Bouquet Garni
½ cup Crème Fraîche (recipe
    page 69)
¼ cup madeira or sherry

Cut veal into 4 portions; pound between waxed paper to ¼-inch thickness. On each place slice of ham and hard-cooked egg. Roll up; secure with string. Coat rolls with flour. In skillet melt butter or margarine. Cook rolls in melted butter till lightly browned on all sides. Combine bouillon granules and ¾ cup *water;* add to skillet along with mushrooms, green onion, and Bouquet Garni. Bring to boiling; reduce heat. Cover; simmer 25 minutes or till rolls are tender, turning once. Remove Bouquet Garni. Stir in Crème Fraîche and wine. Heat through but do not boil. Serves 4.

Bouquet Garni: Combine 1 tablespoon dried *parsley flakes*, 1 teaspoon dried *basil*, 1 teaspoon dried *rosemary*, 1 teaspoon dried *oregano*, 1 *bay leaf*, 6 *peppercorns*, and 1 clove *garlic*. Place in a 6-inch square of cheesecloth; secure with string.

Marie-Christine Ellias
St. Germaine-les-Corbeil, France

NUT TORTE

1½ cups all-purpose flour
½ cup sugar
⅓ cup butter or margarine
1 beaten egg yolk
½ teaspoon vanilla
4 cups pecans, walnuts,
    or almonds
3 beaten eggs
½ cup sugar
⅓ cup all-purpose flour
⅓ cup butter or margarine,
    melted
2 tablespoons rum
¼ cup chopped pecans,
    walnuts, or almonds
½ cup sieved apricot preserves

For pastry, in bowl stir together 1½ cups flour, ½ cup sugar, and ⅛ teaspoon *salt*. Cut in ⅓ cup butter or margarine till crumbly. Combine egg yolk, 1 tablespoon *water,* and vanilla. Add to crumb mixture; mix well. Pat onto bottom and 1 inch up sides of 9-inch springform pan. Bake in 325° oven for 20 minutes. Cool slightly. In blender container or food processor bowl process 4 cups nuts, 1 cup at a time, till ground. Combine ground nuts, beaten eggs, ½ cup sugar, ⅓ cup flour, the ⅓ cup melted butter or margarine, and rum. Spread evenly in crust. Sprinkle with chopped nuts. Bake in 350° oven for 40 minutes. Spoon preserves over top to glaze. Cool 30 minutes. Loosen sides of cake from pan with spatula, then remove sides of pan. Cool completely. Makes 16 servings.

Martine Foucher
Carcassonne, France

CRAB SOUFFLÉ

¼ cup butter or margarine
½ cup all-purpose flour
⅛ teaspoon nutmeg
⅛ teaspoon pepper
    Pinch saffron (optional)
2 cups milk
1 cup shredded process
    Gruyère cheese (4 ounces)
1 5½- or 6-ounce can
    crab meat, drained, flaked,
    and cartilage removed
6 egg yolks
6 stiff-beaten egg whites

Attach foil collar to 2-quart soufflé
dish. For collar measure enough foil
to go around dish plus 2-inch overlap. Fold foil in thirds lengthwise.
Lightly butter one side. With buttered side in, position foil around
dish, letting collar extend 2½ inches
above dish; fasten with tape.

In a saucepan melt butter or margarine; stir in flour, pepper, nutmeg, and saffron, if desired. Add
milk all at once. Cook and stir till
thickened and bubbly. Cook and 1
to 2 minutes more. Stir in cheese till
melted. Remove from heat. Stir in
crabmeat. In small mixer bowl beat
egg yolks till thick and lemon col-
ored (5 minutes). Gradually add
cheese mixture, stirring constantly.
Cool slightly. Fold into egg whites.
Turn into prepared soufflé dish.
Bake in 325° oven 45 to 55 minutes or till knife inserted near center
comes out clean. Serve immediately.
Makes 6 servings.

Rosemary Canaby
Limoux, France

POTATO PIE

4 medium potatoes,
    thinly sliced
2 large onions, sliced
    Pastry for 2-crust 9-inch pie
2 tablespoons butter
1 cup Crème Fraîche (recipe
    below)

In bowl toss together potatoes, onions, 1 teaspoon *salt*, and ¼ teaspoon *pepper*. Turn into pastry-lined
9-inch pie plate. Dot with butter.
Adjust top crust. Seal and flute
edge. Cut slits for escape of steam.
Bake in 375° oven for 55 to 60
minutes or till potatoes are tender.
Cut into wedges to serve. Dollop
with Crème Fraîche. Serves 8.

Odette Belot
Vitry sur Seine, France

CRÈME FRAÎCHE

2 cups whipping cream
¼ cup cultured buttermilk

In small saucepan heat whipping
cream to between 90° and 100°.
Pour into small bowl. Stir in buttermilk. Cover; let stand at room temperature for 18 to 24 hours, or till
mixture is thickened. Do not stir.
Store in covered container in refrigerator up to 1 week. Makes 2 cups.

To replenish the supply, substitute ¼ cup of the Crème Fraîche for
the buttermilk in the recipe above.

Germany

German cooking has a hearty "meat and potatoes" emphasis, but it's full of unexpected delights, too. The Germans know a hundred ways to make sausage and almost as many ways to fix sauerkraut. Herbs are used sparingly, yet no one could call the food bland. Germans like the sweet-sour taste of fruit and meat or fruit and vegetable combinations.

German beer is excellent but tastes slightly different in each city, since breweries supply only their local area.

The custom of eating five meals a day is still observed by many families. A light breakfast is followed around eleven by a more substantial second breakfast. The large meal of the day is eaten at noon. About 5 p.m. work stops for coffee and pastry, at home or at a cafe. Supper is very light.

BAVARIAN DOUGHNUT PUFFS

3¾ to 4¼ cups all-purpose flour
2 packages active dry yeast
1 cup milk
¼ cup sugar
¼ cup butter or margarine
¼ cup rum
  Few drops rum extract (optional)
2 eggs
  Shortening or cooking oil for deep-fat frying
  Sifted powdered sugar

In mixer bowl combine *2 cups* of the flour and the yeast. Heat milk, sugar, butter or margarine, and ½ teaspoon *salt* just till warm (115° to 120°); stir constantly. Add rum and rum extract, if desired. Add to flour mixture; add eggs. Beat at low speed of electric mixer for ½ minute, scraping bowl. Beat 3 minutes at high speed. Stir in as much remaining flour as you can mix in with a spoon. Turn out onto lightly floured surface. Knead in enough remaining flour to make a moderately soft dough that is smooth and elastic (3 to 5 minutes). Place in greased bowl; turn once. Cover; let rise in warm place till double (about 1 hour). Punch down. Cover and chill for 2 to 3 hours. Divide dough into 36 portions; flatten to round flat shape. Cover; let rise till light (20 to 30 minutes). Fry a few at a time in deep hot fat (375°) about ½ to 1 minute per side or till golden. Drain; dust with powdered sugar. Makes 36.

Centa Gerner
Petersbuch, Germany

FISH AND CLAM CHOWDER

1 pound fish fillets
4 ounces salt pork
2 cups diced potatoes
2 stalks celery, chopped
3 tablespoons sliced green onion
1 14½-ounce can chicken broth
3 cups milk
3 tablespoons all-purpose flour
1 cup whipping cream
1 6½-ounce can minced clams
1 10-ounce package frozen chopped spinach, cooked and well drained

Thaw fish, if frozen. Cut into ½-inch pieces. Chop salt pork; in Dutch oven cook till brown. Drain, reserving 3 tablespoons drippings. Set salt pork aside. Add potatoes, celery, and green onion to reserved drippings. Cook till onion is tender. Add broth. Cover; cook 10 minutes or till potatoes are tender. Add fish and *2½ cups* of the milk. Bring just to boiling. Reduce heat; simmer 3 minutes or till fish is done. Shake remaining cold milk with flour. Stir into chowder. Cook and stir till bubbly. Cook 1 minute more. Add cream, *undrained* clams, spinach, salt pork, ¼ teaspoon *salt*, ¼ teaspoon *pepper*, and dash bottled *hot pepper sauce*. Heat through. Serves 8 to 10.

Marianne Gronau
Amberg, Germany

Rich, creamy, and subtly flavored, Fish and Clam Chowder is homemade soup at its best. Serve it for lunch or supper with German-style rye bread and a fruit salad.

Germany

SMOKED PORK CHOPS WITH SAUERKRAUT

- 2 tablespoons lard or shortening
- 1 medium onion, chopped
- 1 16-ounce can sauerkraut, drained
- 2 apples, peeled, cored, and sliced
- ½ teaspoon beef bouillon granules
- 4 fully cooked smoked pork chops, cut ½ inch thick (1½ pounds)
- 2 medium onions, sliced
- 1 small carrot, sliced
- 1 bay leaf
- 2 peppercorns
- 1 tablespoon cornstarch
- ½ cup dry white wine
- ½ cup sour cream
  Snipped parsley
  Boiled potatoes

In skillet melt lard or shortening. Cook chopped onion and sauerkraut in hot fat till onion is tender. Add apple slices, 1 cup *water,* and bouillon granules. Cover and cook over medium-low heat for 30 minutes. Meanwhile, place chops, sliced onions, carrot, bay leaf, and peppercorns in 12x7½x2-inch baking dish. Add ¼ cup *water.* Cover; bake in 350° oven for 30 minutes. Remove chops and keep warm. Strain pan juices from meat, discarding vegetables and seasonings. Skim off fat. Combine cornstarch and *2 tablespoons* of the wine. In small saucepan combine pan juices, cornstarch mixture, and remaining wine. Cook and stir till mixture thickens and bubbles. Cook and stir 2 minutes more. Stir half the sauce into sour cream. Return to mixture in saucepan. Heat through. Place sauerkraut mixture on serving plate; top with chops. Sprinkle with parsley. Pour sauce into bowl; pass with meat. Serve with boiled potatoes. Serves 4.

Birkhild Mensinger
Berlin, Germany

MEATBALLS WITH BUTTERMILK GRAVY

- 1 beaten egg
- ¼ cup milk
- ¼ cup fine dry bread crumbs
- ¾ cup finely chopped onion
- 1½ teaspoons prepared mustard
- 1½ pounds ground beef
- 1 tablespoon cooking oil
- 1 medium onion, sliced
- ¼ cup all-purpose flour
- 2 cups buttermilk
  Hot cooked noodles or spaetzle

Combine egg and milk; stir in crumbs, chopped onion, mustard, 1 teaspoon *salt,* and dash *pepper.* Add meat; mix well. Shape into 30 1½-inch meatballs. In large skillet cook meatballs in hot oil, turning often, 25 minutes or till done. Remove meatballs, reserving 2 tablespoons drippings. Add sliced onion; cook till tender. Stir together flour, ¼ teaspoon *salt,* and buttermilk; add to skillet. Cook and stir till thickened and bubbly. Reduce heat. Return meatballs to skillet. Cook 2 minutes. Serve with hot cooked noodles or spaetzle. Makes 6 servings.

Jutta Stegemann
Munich, Germany

SAUERBRATEN

For an authentic German touch serve spaetzle with the Sauerbraten. They're like tiny dumplings, delicious with the tender meat and tangy gravy--

1 teaspoon peppercorns
2 bay leaves
6 whole cloves
4 juniper berries (optional)
1 cup red wine vinegar
1 4-pound boneless beef round
    rump roast
2 medium onions, sliced
2 stalks celery, sliced
1 carrot, sliced
2 tablespoons cooking oil
2 teaspoons instant beef
    bouillon granules
2 slices pumpernickel,
    crumbled
⅓ cup raisins
⅓ cup all-purpose flour
½ cup red wine
    Hot cooked noodles or
    spaetzle

In a 6-inch square of cheesecloth combine peppercorns, bay leaves, whole cloves, and juniper berries, if desired. Secure spices in the cheesecloth bag. Set aside.

In saucepan combine vinegar, 4 cups *water*, 2 teaspoons *salt*, and the cheesecloth bag of spices. Bring to boiling; cool to room temperature. Place meat in plastic bag in large bowl; add onions, celery, carrot, and cheesecloth bag of spices. Pour vinegar mixture over meat. Tie bag closed. Refrigerate 3 to 4 days, turning meat occasionally.

Remove meat from marinade, reserving vegetables and marinade and discarding cheesecloth bag. Pat meat dry with paper toweling. In Dutch oven brown meat on all sides in hot oil. Add vegetables from marinade, beef bouillon granules, crumbled pumpernickel, and *3 cups* of the reserved marinade. Bring to boiling; reduce heat. Cover; simmer 1½ hours, turning meat occasionally. Add raisins; simmer 30 minutes more or till meat is tender.

Remove meat and vegetables to serving plate; keep warm. Reserve 3 cups cooking liquid and vegetables in Dutch oven. Combine flour and red wine; stir into juices in pan. Cook and stir till thickened and bubbly. Cook and stir 2 minutes more. Spoon some gravy over meat and vegetables. To serve, slice meat. Serve with noodles or spaetzle. Spoon some gravy atop; pass remaining. Makes 12 servings.

Christa Bauer
Usingen, Germany

SPAETZLE

   2 cups all-purpose flour
   1 teaspoon salt
   2 eggs
  ¾ cup milk

In a mixing bowl combine flour and salt. Mix eggs and milk; stir into flour mixture. Place batter in coarse-sieved deep-fat frying basket or colander with ¼-inch holes. Hold over kettle of boiling salted water. Press the batter through the deep-fat frying basket or colander with the back of a wooden spoon or rubber spatula. If the dough is too thick to push through, thin it with a little milk. Cook and stir for 5 minutes; drain. Keep warm.

MEDITE

RANEAN

Italy

Italy is identified not only for its pasta and pizza, but other national specialties such as sausages, prosciutto, and cheeses like Gorgonzola, Parmesan, and ricotta.

Two basic cooking styles are prevalent in Italy. In the south, pasta is the staple, solid or tubular-shaped, made without eggs and served with robust tomato sauces seasoned with olive oil and garlic.

To the north, dishes are milder and sauces are made with fresh cream instead of tomatoes. Pasta is usually ribbon-shaped and contains eggs. And often, beans, rice, and polenta (made from cornmeal) are served in place of pasta.

But Italian kitchens both north and south are stocked with mellow and sharp cheeses and fresh herbs such as parsley, rosemary, basil, oregano, and mint.

EGGPLANT PARMIGIANA

½ cup chopped onion
2 cloves garlic, minced
1 tablespoon butter
1 16-ounce can tomatoes, cut up
⅓ cup tomato paste
2 tablespoons snipped parsley
2 teaspoons dried basil, crushed
½ teaspoon dried thyme, crushed
2 medium eggplants, peeled and cut crosswise into ½-inch thick slices
Cooking oil or olive oil
½ cup grated Parmesan cheese
6 ounces sliced mozzarella cheese

Cook onion and garlic in butter till onion is tender but not brown. Stir in tomatoes, tomato paste, parsley, basil, thyme, ¼ teaspoon *salt,* and ¼ teaspoon *pepper.* Bring to boilng; reduce heat. Boil gently, uncovered, about 15 minutes or till desired consistency (should have about 2½ cups), stirring occasionally. Sprinkle eggplant slices lightly with *salt;* drain for 30 minutes. Pat dry with paper toweling. In large skillet fry eggplant in hot oil till golden. Spread about ½ *cup* tomato sauce in bottom of 12x7½x2-inch baking dish. Arrange a single layer of eggplant in bottom, cutting slices to fit. Top with *half* the remaining sauce and *half* the Parmesan and mozzarella cheeses. Repeat layers. Bake, uncovered, in 400° oven 20 minutes or till heated through. Serves 8.

Gianfranca Ceritelli Fiorini
Bologna, Italy

MINESTRONE

½ cup dry great northern beans or navy beans
1½ cups shredded cabbage
1 medium potato, peeled and cubed (1 cup)
4 teaspoons instant chicken bouillon granules
1 large clove garlic, minced
1 bay leaf
1 teaspoon dried basil, crushed
2 tablespoons olive oil
2 tablespoons all-purpose flour
2 tablespoons snipped parsley
Grated Parmesan cheese

Rinse the dry beans. In a large saucepan combine beans and 4 cups *water.* Bring to boiling; reduce heat and simmer for 2 minutes. Remove from heat; cover and let stand 1 hour. (*Or,* cover and soak beans in the water overnight.) Drain; add 5 *cups* fresh water. Return to boiling; reduce heat. Simmer, covered, for 1 to 1¼ hours or till beans are tender. Stir in cabbage, potato, bouillon granules, garlic, bay leaf, basil, ½ teaspoon *salt,* and ¼ teaspoon *pepper.* Bring to boiling. Reduce heat; cover and simmer for 25 to 30 minutes or till vegetables are just tender.

In a small saucepan heat olive oil; blend in flour. Cook and stir over medium-low heat for 7 to 8 minutes or till a rich dark brown; cool slightly. Stir in about *1 cup* of the hot soup liquid; return all to the soup. Bring to boiling; cook 1 minute more. Stir in parsley. Sprinkle each serving with grated Parmesan cheese, if desired. Makes 4 servings.

Grazia Martellani
Trieste, Italy

ANTIPASTO VOLANTE

Volante means "flying" and this antipasto gets a flying start from canned and prepared foods--

4 ounces smoked red salmon,
 thinly sliced
1 3¾-ounce can tuna
1 3¾-ounce can sardines in oil
 Lettuce leaves (optional)
6 pickled artichoke hearts
 or 6 small ribs of celery
 Pitted ripe olives
3 hard-cooked eggs, cut into
 wedges
½ of 15-ounce can garbanzo
 beans, drained
1½ cups shelled cooked shrimp
2 tablespoons olive oil
2 tablespoons snipped parsley
1 lemon, cut into wedges

Chill fish, if desired. On a lettuce-lined platter arrange chunks of salmon, tuna, sardines, artichoke hearts or celery, pitted ripe olives, wedges of hard-cooked egg, and garbanzo beans. Toss together the shelled shrimp, the olive oil, ⅛ teaspoon *salt,* and ⅛ teaspoon *pepper.* Arrange on platter. Sprinkle with snipped parsley; squeeze lemon over all. Makes 6 appetizer servings.

Emanuela Petteno Zanon
Venice, Italy

The word antipasto means "before the meal," and is an appetizer course intended to whet the appetite. Creatively arranged, antipastos include endless combinations of fish, meats, cheeses, vegetables, and fruits. Pictured here is Antipasto Volante.

Spain

The Turkish and Arab influence in the Mediterranean, combined with the characteristic flavors of garlic and olive oil, pervade the Spanish cuisine. Abundantly available foods such as rice, figs, citrus fruits, almonds, and spices are prevalent ingredients in the country's local cooking.

Tomatoes, red and green peppers, and chocolate came from Spain's Latin American conquests and serve as reminders of its past.

Spain's classic dish, Paella, is a hearty combination of sausage, chicken, seafood, rice, and vegetables, seasoned with saffron and olive oil. It was first made in Valencia and is named after the double-handled shallow baking pan in which Spanish cooks have always prepared it.

COD AND POTATO BAKE

    8 ounces salt cod
    4 medium potatoes, peeled and
        thinly sliced (1 cup)
    1 medium onion, chopped
    2 tablespoons cooking oil
    2 tablespoons butter
    2 tablespoons all-purpose flour
    1 cup milk
    3 stiff-beaten egg whites
    ½ cup whipping cream,
        whipped
    2 tablespoons snipped parsley

Soak cod in enough water to cover for several hours or overnight, changing water several times. Drain fish; cut into small pieces. Cook cod, covered, in *boiling water* about 10 minutes or till tender; drain and rinse. Cool; flake with fork. In large skillet cook potatoes and onion in hot oil till slightly browned, stirring constantly. Remove from heat. Add ½ cup *water*. Cook potato mixture, covered, over low heat for 15 to 20 minutes or till potatoes are tender. Set aside.

In a saucepan melt butter. Stir in flour, ¼ teaspoon *salt*, and dash *pepper*. Add milk all at once. Cook and stir till bubbly. Cook and stir 1 to 2 minutes more. Set aside. Toss together cod and potato mixture. Turn into a 10x6x2-inch baking dish. Pour sauce evenly over potato mixture. Fold together egg whites and whipped cream; spread atop mixture in baking dish. Bake in 400° oven for 13 to 15 minutes or till golden and heated through. Sprinkle with parsley. Serves 4 to 6.

Maria Gregoria Moreno-Vilches
Badajoz, Spain

CHOCOLATE CREAM

    2 4-ounce packages sweet
        cooking chocolate, coarsely
        chopped
    ⅓ cup butter or margarine
    4 beaten egg yolks
    4 stiff-beaten egg whites
    2 tablespoons sugar
        Finely chopped orange peel
        (optional)
        Whipped cream (optional)

In a small heavy saucepan melt together chocolate and butter or margarine over low heat, stirring constantly. Gradually stir about half the hot chocolate mixture into the beaten egg yolks; return all to saucepan. Cook and stir over low heat 2 minutes more or till very thick and glossy. Remove from heat; cool to room temperature.

Beat egg whites to soft peaks; gradually add sugar, beating till stiff peaks form. Fold a small amount of the egg whites into chocolate mixture to lighten. Fold chocolate mixture into remaining beaten egg whites. Spoon mixture into dessert glasses, using about ¼ cup mixture in each. Cover; chill several hours or overnight. Garnish with chopped orange peel or whipped cream, if desired. Makes 10 servings.

Angeles Pina Escudero
Murcia, Spain

Chocolate Cream is a sinfully rich dessert that's delightfully easy to make. Fresh-brewed cups of espresso are perfect companions.

FAR

EAST

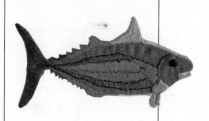

Japan

Each Japanese meal is intended to be a feast to the eyes as well as the palate. Arrangement of foods and garnishes is vital. Seasonings are delicate and fragrant. Japanese housewives shop each day because their kitchens have little storage space and because freshness and quality of foods are very important. Foods are eaten only in their peak season. First-of-the-season strawberries, mushrooms, and melons are eagerly awaited. The choicest are specially packed and given as gifts.

The Japanese "farm" the sea, using dozens of varieties of fish, seafood, and seaweed. They also make use of the tender sprouts and leaf tips of many plants.

Each diner's meal is served individually, each food in a separate dish, and the rice is usually eaten last. Many mildly seasoned dishes are served with a potent sauce into which each bite is dipped before eating.

BROILED GINGER PORK

Thin slices of pork absorb the sherry-flavored marinade quickly, then broil even faster to make a delicious oriental dish--

- ¾ **pound boneless pork**
- ¼ **cup dry sherry**
- ¼ **cup soy sauce**
- 2 **tablespoons sugar**
- 2 **tablespoons vinegar**
- 1 **teaspoon grated gingerroot**
  Cooking oil

Partially freeze pork; slice thinly. Place pork slices in shallow bowl. Combine dry sherry, soy sauce, sugar, vinegar, and gingerroot; pour over pork. Marinate 15 minutes at room temperature, stirring occasionally. Drain meat, reserving marinade. In small saucepan cook marinade over medium-high heat till reduced to about ⅓ cup. Brush broiler rack with oil. Arrange meat on unheated rack in broiler pan. Broil 3 inches from the heat for 5 to 7 minutes or till done, brushing twice with reduced marinade. Makes 4 servings.

Sumiko Kiyokawa
Osaka, Japan

SUKIYAKI

- 12 **dried mushrooms**
- 1 **pound beef tenderloin**
- 2 **ounces transparent noodles**
- ¾ **cup sake or dry sherry**
- ½ **cup beef broth**
- ½ **cup soy sauce**
- ½ **cup water**
- 3 **tablespoons sugar**
- 6 **green onions, bias sliced into 1-inch pieces (1 cup)**
- 5 **cups sliced Chinese cabbage**
- 2 **tablespoons cooking oil**

In small bowl soak mushrooms in enough warm water to cover for 30 minutes; squeeze to drain well. Remove stems; halve large mushrooms. Partially freeze beef. Slice very thinly across the grain into bite-size pieces. Soak noodles in cold water for 30 minutes till rehydrated. Drain. Combine sake, beef broth, soy sauce, water, and sugar; set aside. Preheat an electric frypan or wok; add oil. Quickly stir-fry meat till brown; remove. Add beef broth mixture; bring to boiling. Place the mushrooms, cabbage, transparent noodles, green onion, and the meat in separate areas of pan; *do not mix.* Return to boiling. Simmer, uncovered, for 1 minute. Serve immediately. Serves 6.

浜 田 芳 子
Yoshiko Hamada
Tokyo, Japan

Arrange the ingredients for Sukiyaki on a tray, then cook at the table in an electric wok or frypan. The meat and vegetables cook quickly and retain all their natural fresh flavor and texture.

Japan

TEPPENYAKI

A "teppen" is the large griddle on which the Japanese cook this dish. An electric griddle makes a good substitute for tableside cooking--

**12 fresh or frozen large shrimp
½ pound boneless beef sirloin
    or top round steak
1 whole medium chicken
    breast, skinned,
    halved lengthwise, and
    boned
3 or 4 desired vegetables*,
    drained and patted dry
Cooking oil
Soy-Ginger Sauce
Hot Mustard Sauce
Hot cooked rice**

Thaw shrimp, if frozen. Shell and devein shrimp. Partially freeze beef and chicken; thinly slice across the grain into bite-size strips. Toss beef and chicken separately with a little oil. Arrange beef, chicken, shrimp, and vegetables on a large platter.

Heat electric griddle at the table; brush on about 2 tablespoons oil. To cook vegetables start with those that take longer (carrot, leeks, green pepper) and end with vegetables requiring less time (mushrooms, pea pods, bean sprouts). Cook *half* of each vegetable, one at a time, stir-frying till vegetable is crisp-tender; add oil as needed. Push cooked vegetables to side of griddle. Transfer vegetables to platter.

Add *half* the beef, chicken, and shrimp to griddle; stir-fry, keeping separate, 1 to 3 minutes or till meat is desired doneness and shrimp are pink. Transfer to platter; serve at once. Repeat with remaining vegetables and meat. Serve with Soy-Ginger Sauce, Hot Mustard Sauce, and hot cooked rice. Serves 6.

*Note: Vegetable options: 2 cups cut-up Chinese cabbage or spinach; 1 cup thinly sliced carrot; 2 leeks, sliced crosswise; 1 cup green pepper cut into strips; 1 cup sliced water chestnuts; 1 cup sliced fresh mushrooms; 1 cup fresh pea pods; 1 cup fresh bean sprouts.

Soy-Ginger Sauce: Combine 3 tablespoons *soy sauce*, 2 tablespoons *rice vinegar* or *white vinegar*, and ⅛ teaspoon *ground ginger*.

Hot Mustard Sauce: Combine ¼ cup *dry mustard* and 1½ teaspoons *sugar*. Stir in 2 tablespoons *water* and 2 tablespoons *soy sauce* till smooth.

YAKIMONO

Yakimono means "broiled things," a good description of this Japanese favorite--

**8 ounces fresh or frozen
    scallops
½ cup soy sauce
¼ cup sake or dry sherry
1 tablespoon sugar
1 teaspoon grated gingerroot
8 ounces boneless beef sirloin
    or top round steak, cut
    into 1-inch cubes
12 whole green onions, cut into
    2-inch lengths**

Thaw scallops, if frozen. In saucepan combine soy sauce, sake, ¼ cup *water*, sugar, and gingerroot. Boil 1 minute; cool. Cut up any large scallops. Marinate scallops, beef, and green onions in soy mixture for 15 minutes at room temperature, turning once. Drain, reserving marinade. On skewers alternately thread scallops, beef, and onions. Grill over *hot* coals 8 to 10 minutes or till done; turn and brush occasionally with reserved marinade. Serves 4.

GREEN BEANS WITH MISO DRESSING

Miso, a pastelike flavoring made from soybeans, is used in soups and sauces. It's available in both light and dark forms. Try it in this modified version of a Japanese classic--

3 cups fresh green beans,
    bias sliced into
    1-inch pieces, or two 9-
    ounce packages frozen
    cut green beans
Miso Dressing
Toasted sesame seed
Lemon peel strips

In a covered saucepan cook cut green beans in a small amount of boiling water 20 to 30 minutes or till crisp-tender. (If using frozen green beans, cook according to package directions, omitting salt in cooking water.) Drain well. Toss with Miso Dressing; chill well. Remove from refrigerator about ½ hour before serving time to bring to room temperature. Pass toasted sesame seed and lemon peel strips. Makes 6 servings.

Miso Dressing: In a small bowl combine 1 *egg yolk* with ¼ cup *white miso* (white bean paste). Stir in 1 tablespoon *sake* or *dry sherry,* 1 tablespoon *water,* and 1 teaspoon *sugar*; mix well. Makes about ½ cup sauce.

FRIED CHICKEN WINGS

Cornstarch is used often in Japan in coatings for frying. It makes a light, crispy crust--

1 pound chicken wings
⅓ cup sake or dry sherry
3 tablespoons soy sauce
1 teaspoon grated gingerroot
¼ cup cornstarch
    Cooking oil for deep-fat
    frying
4 thin lemon slices

Cut chicken wings at joints; discard wing tips. In bowl combine sake or sherry, soy sauce, and gingerroot. Place chicken in plastic bag set in bowl; pour marinade over chicken. Close bag. Marinate in refrigerator several hours or overnight, turning occasionally. Drain chicken; pat dry with paper toweling. Coat chicken wings with cornstarch. Fry, 3 or 4 pieces at a time, in deep hot fat (365°) for about 4 minutes. Drain on paper toweling. Remove chicken to serving plate; garnish with lemon slices. Makes 4 appetizer servings.

S. Yoshinaga

Sachiko Yoshinaga
Tokyo, Japan

Malaysia

The legendary "spice islands" included the area that is now Malaysia. First the Arabs, then the Portuguese and Dutch traded with the Malays to obtain cinnamon, cloves, cumin, ginger, and other fragrant spices. Even today Malay food is spicy and hot with chilies. Their sauces include the original "kechop," which, despite the name, contains no tomatoes.

Malays eat rice at every meal but eat more seafood and less pork than other Asians because most Malays are Muslims. They love sweet, rich desserts to end the meal.

Satay is a Malaysian favorite that is winning international acclaim. Cubed meat on skewers is basted with soy sauce and oil as it grills, then served with a hot sauce of chilies, spices, and peanuts. At the end of the work day in Malaysian cities, food stalls serving satay are set up to cater to evening strollers.

FRIED BEEF BUNDLES

  1 small onion, cut into wedges
  3 red chili peppers, seeded
  1 clove garlic
  1 thin slice gingerroot
  ½ pound ground beef
  1 large carrot, shredded
  1 turnip, shredded
  ¼ teaspoon salt
  2 beaten eggs
 10 egg roll skins
    Cooking oil for deep-fat
      frying
    Chinese mustard, sweet-sour
      sauce, or chili sauce

In food processor fitted with a steel blade combine onion, chili peppers, garlic, and ginger; process till almost smooth. Set aside. In skillet combine ground beef, carrot, turnip, and salt. Cook, uncovered, over high heat till meat is browned, stirring frequently. Drain off fat. Stir in onion mixture. Remove from heat; stir in eggs. Place egg roll skin with one point toward you. Spoon ¼ cup of filling diagonally across and just below center of skin. Fold bottom point of skin over filling; tuck point under filling. Fold side corners over, forming envelope shape. Roll up toward remaining corner; moisten point and press firmly to seal. Repeat with remaining egg roll skins and filling. Fry bundles, a few at a time, in deep hot oil (365°) about 2 minutes or till golden brown. Drain on paper toweling. Serve with Chinese mustard, sweet-sour sauce, or chili sauce. Makes 10.

Janet Chong Bee Lay
Tapah, Malaysia

PINEAPPLE PASTRIES

  ½ of a medium pineapple
  ½ cup sugar
  ⅓ cup water
  ½ cup butter or margarine
  2 cups all-purpose flour
  2 beaten egg yolks
  ½ teaspoon vanilla
  5 to 6 tablespoons cold water
  2 slightly beaten egg whites

Peel pineapple; remove eyes and core. Chop pineapple to make 1½ cups. In saucepan combine pineapple, sugar, and ⅓ cup water. Bring to boiling; reduce heat to medium and boil gently about 25 minutes or till thickened, stirring occasionally. (Watch closely last 5 minutes to prevent sticking.) Cool.

Meanwhile, in bowl cut butter into flour till mixture is crumbly. Add egg yolks and vanilla; stir till well combined. Sprinkle 1 tablespoon of the cold water over part of mixture; gently toss with fork. Push to side of bowl. Repeat till all is moistened. Form dough into ball. Cover; chill 1 hour. Divide dough in half. On lightly floured surface roll each half to 10x10-inch square. Cut into sixteen 2½-inch squares. Spoon about *1 teaspoon* pineapple filling diagonally in center of each square. Bring up two side corners; overlap slightly. Place on ungreased baking sheet. Brush lightly with egg white to seal. Bake in 400° oven for 10 to 12 minutes till golden brown. Cool on wire rack. Makes 32.

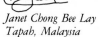

Chan Lin Yeng
Telok Anson, Malaysia

MALAYSIAN STIR-FRIED CHICKEN

2 tablespoons cooking oil
4 small onions, thinly sliced
4 fresh red or green hot chili
    peppers, seeded and
    thinly sliced
2 whole chicken breasts,
    skinned, boned, and
    cut into 1-inch pieces
¾ cup cold water
1 tablespoon sugar
1 tablespoon cornstarch
2 tablespoons lime juice
2 tablespoons soy sauce
    Hot cooked rice

Preheat skillet or wok over high heat; add cooking oil. Stir-fry onions 2 minutes. Add chilies; stir-fry 30 seconds. Add chicken pieces; stir-fry 2 minutes. Combine water, sugar, cornstarch, lime juice, and soy sauce. Add to mixture in skillet. Cook and stir till thickened and bubbly. Cook and stir 2 minutes longer. Serve with hot cooked rice. Makes 3 or 4 servings.

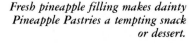

Jacqueline Raj
Kuala Lumpar, Malaysia

Fresh pineapple filling makes dainty Pineapple Pastries a tempting snack or dessert.

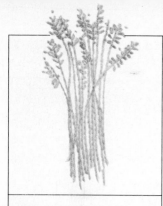

Thailand

Thailand is the only country in southeast Asia which has never been a colony and this independence has preserved its unique cuisine. Many of the finest professional cooks are women, a custom that began because only women could be employed in the palace apartments of the Siamese king's wives.

The first preparation step for any Thai dish is grinding together with mortar and pestle the garlic, hot chilies, and spices to form a seasoning paste. Cooking is done ahead of time and foods are served at room temperature. Dinner begins with a soup, followed by rice and two or more dishes with spicy gravy, one of which is fish or seafood, and a side dish or two. Desserts are generally fresh fruits. In restaurants these are often intricately carved to make a bouquet of edible flowers. Sweets are popular snacks.

PANANG MEATBALLS

You can usually find bottled red curry paste at Thai and oriental grocery stores. Canned coconut milk also is available and can be used in this recipe--

    1 pound ground beef
    3 tablespoons all-purpose flour
    2 tablespoons cooking oil
    1 to 2 tablepoons red curry
      paste
    2 tablespoons peanut butter
    1 tablespoon sugar
    1 tablespoon fish sauce
 1⅓ cups Coconut Milk
    Hot cooked rice

Shape ground beef into 24 1-inch balls; coat lightly with flour. In skillet cook meatballs in hot oil 10 to 15 minutes or till brown, shaking pan frequently to keep meatballs round. Drain meatballs, reserving 1 tablespoon drippings. Add curry paste to reserved drippings; cook and stir over low heat for 2 to 3 minutes. Stir in peanut butter, sugar, and fish sauce; mix well. Add coconut milk. Bring to boiling; reduce heat. Add meatballs to coconut milk mixture. Cover; cook 3 to 5 minutes till meatballs are heated through. Serve with hot cooked rice. Makes 4 servings.
  Coconut Milk: Stir together ⅔ cup *unsweetened grated coconut* and 1⅓ cups boiling *water;* let stand 5 minutes. Place mixture in blender container. Cover; blend 1 minute. Makes 1⅓ cups.

Panida Tongpradith
Panida Tongpradith
Bangkok, Thailand

THAI SHRIMP SALAD

Look for lemon grass in Oriental food stores; if unavailable, substitute ¼ teaspoon shredded lemon peel--

    3 cups water
    1 pound fresh or frozen shrimp
      in shell
    2 tablespoons sliced
      green onion
    1 tablespoon finely chopped
      lemon grass
  ¾ teaspoon chopped seeded red
      chili pepper
    1 clove garlic, minced
    1 tablespoon lemon or
      lime juice
    1 tablespoon fish sauce
    2 teaspoons oil
    Lettuce

In saucepan bring water to boiling. Add shrimp. Simmer 2 to 3 minutes or till shrimp turn pink. Drain; shell and devein. In bowl combine green onion, lemon grass, chili pepper, garlic, lemon or lime juice, fish sauce, and oil. Mix well. Add shrimp; toss to coat well. Cover and chill. Toss again before serving. Serve on lettuce-lined plate. Makes 3 or 4 servings.

Oraval Paethong
Oraval Paethong
Bangkok, Thailand

For a taste of summer any time of year, serve Thai Shrimp Salad. It gets its zip from hot chili peppers and lemon grass.

SOUTH

PACIFIC

Australia & New Zealand

The first settlers "down under" were British, and even today many Australians and New Zealanders enjoy the simple, substantial meals which originated with their pioneers. But nearby Oriental and Indonesian cuisines have added spice, as has the influence of later immigrants from many countries.

Beef is the mainstay meat in Australia and a favorite way to serve it is carpetbagger steak, a thick cut stuffed with raw oysters, then grilled. The seafood is excellent, and the warm coastal areas contribute a wide variety of fruits and vegetables to Australian dinner tables. A pleasing surprise to visitors to Australia is the fine wine made here.

In New Zealand lamb is more popular than beef. The traditional holiday dish is "colonial goose" (stuffed lamb served with tart sauce). Teatime brings a feast of home-baked cakes and tarts.

KIWI CREAM PIE

  1½ cups finely crushed vanilla
      wafers (36 wafers)
  1 teaspoon ground cinnamon
  ⅓ cup butter or margarine,
      melted
  1 envelope unflavored gelatin
  ½ cup cold water
  1 8-ounce carton plain yogurt
  ½ cup sugar
  1 tablespoon lemon juice
  ½ cup whipping cream
  2 kiwi fruit, peeled and sliced
  ½ cup whipping cream

In a mixing bowl combine crushed vanilla wafers, cinnamon, and butter or margarine. Press onto bottom and sides of a 9-inch pie plate to form a firm, even crust. Chill about 1 hour. Meanwhile, in a small saucepan soften gelatin in cold water. Cook and stir over medium heat till gelatin is dissolved. Cool. Beat together yogurt, sugar, and lemon juice; stir in the cooled gelatin mixture. Chill till partially set, stirring occasionally. Beat ½ cup whipping cream till soft peaks form. Fold whipped cream into gelatin mixture. Chill till mixture mounds when spooned. Turn into chilled crust. Cover and chill several hours or till set. Just before serving, arrange some of the sliced kiwi around edge of pie. Beat ½ cup whipping cream to soft peaks. Spoon into center of pie; garnish with remaining sliced kiwi. Makes 8 servings.

Lenor Kwok
Wellington, New Zealand

PAVLOVA

  3 egg whites
  1½ cups sugar
  1½ teaspoons vanilla
  1½ teaspoons vinegar
  1 cup whipping cream
  ½ teaspoon vanilla
  4 cups sliced fresh fruit,
      such as kiwi
      fruit, strawberries,
      bananas, peaches, or
      pineapple chunks

Bring egg whites to room temperature. Line a baking sheet with foil. Using an 8x1½-inch cake pan as a guide, draw a circle on the foil. In a large mixer bowl combine egg whites, sugar, 1½ teaspoons vanilla, vinegar, and ¼ cup *boiling water.* Beat about 12 minutes, scraping bowl constantly, till stiff peaks form and mixture holds its shape. Spread egg white mixture over circle on foil. Shape into shell with back of spoon, making the bottom ½ inch thick and the sides 2½ to 3 inches high. Preheat oven to 450°. Place baking sheet in center of oven and turn oven off. Let stand 4 to 5 hours. *Do not open oven door.*

Combine whipping cream and ½ teaspoon vanilla. Beat till soft peaks form. Remove meringue shell from foil; place on serving plate. Spread whipped cream in shell, reserving ½ cup for garnish. Arrange fruit in shell. Mound reserved whipped cream in center of fruit. Cut into wedges. Serve immediately. Makes 8 to 10 servings.

Margaret Wallis
Wellington, New Zealand

SPICY MEAT LOAF

2 slightly beaten eggs
1 11-ounce can tomato bisque
½ cup seasoned fine dry
    bread crumbs
1 medium onion, finely
    chopped
2 teaspoons curry powder
1 pound lean ground beef
1 pound bulk pork sausage
1 tablespoon all-purpose flour
¼ cup water

In bowl combine eggs, *½ cup* of the tomato bisque, bread crumbs, onion, and curry powder. Add ground beef and sausage; mix well. Form meat mixture into 2 loaves about 6x3x3 inches and place in a 13x9x2-inch baking pan. Bake in 350° oven for 1 hour or till done. Transfer meat loaves to platter; keep warm.

For sauce, measure 1 tablespoon pan drippings into saucepan; blend in the flour. Add remaining tomato bisque and water all at once. Cook and stir till thickened and bubbly; cook and stir 1 minute more. Serve sauce with meat loaves. Makes 8 servings.

Helen Lavendar
Southwest Rocks, Australia

Pavlova, named for a famous ballerina, is a fascinating combination of flavors and textures-- tart fruit, billows of whipped cream, and a shell that's crisp on the outside and marshmallowy inside.

Philippines

Philippine cooking owes a debt to the cuisines of Spain and China. Four centuries of Spanish rule brought rich desserts, spicy sausages, and olive oil to Philippine tables. Lucky visitors discover another Spanish gift, the custom of the merienda, a late afternoon meal of cakes, tarts, and sweet fritters. These sweets often are based on "sticky rice", introduced by Chinese merchants, who also taught Filipino cooks to use noodles and soy sauce.

At nearly every meal, including breakfast, Philippine families enjoy dishes that combine sour and salty flavors. The sour taste comes from vinegar or the tamarind fruit, the salty from fish sauce or paste.

The favorite food for snacking here is Lumpia, a lettuce-lined egg roll skin filled with vegetables and meats, and served with a sauce for dipping.

LUMPIA

1 small onion, chopped
2 cloves garlic, minced
2 tablespoons cooking oil
8 ounces cooked pork, diced
½ cup chopped shrimp
½ cup cooked garbanzos
¼ cup chopped cooked ham
2 carrots, cut into julienne strips
½ cup frozen French-style green beans, thawed
1 14-ounce can hearts of palm, drained and chopped
2 cups shredded cabbage
18 egg roll skins
Lettuce leaves
Brown Sauce

Cook onion and garlic in hot oil till tender. Add pork, shrimp, garbanzos, and ham. Simmer, uncovered, 5 minutes, stirring frequently. Add carrots, green beans, hearts of palm, and ¼ cup *water*. Cook, covered, 5 minutes. Stir in cabbage and 1 teaspoon *salt;* cook, covered, 7 minutes or till vegetables are done. Cool. To prepare skins, brush a little cooking oil in large shallow skillet. Cook 1 egg roll skin, on one side only, over medium heat 30 to 45 seconds or till light brown. Turn out onto paper toweling. Repeat with remaining skins, adding oil if needed.

To assemble, place an egg roll skin unbrowned side up with one corner facing you; top with a lettuce leaf and ⅓ cup of vegetable mixture. Roll up, folding in one end of egg roll skin and leaving other end open. Serve immediately with Brown Sauce. Makes 18 rolls.

Brown Sauce: In saucepan stir together ¼ cup *sugar* and 1 tablespoon *cornstarch*; stir in 1 cup *chicken broth* and 2 tablespoons *soy sauce*.

Cook and stir till mixture thickens and bubbles. Cook and stir 2 minutes more. Stir in 1 clove *garlic*, minced. Makes about 1 cup.

Adelina Bassig
Manila, Philippines

COCONUT MACAROON CUPCAKES

1 cup all-purpose flour
1 cup nonfat dry milk powder
½ cup butter or margarine
1 cup sugar
1 egg yolk
⅓ cup evaporated milk
2½ cups flaked coconut

Stir together flour and dry milk powder. In small mixer bowl beat butter or margarine on medium speed for 30 seconds. Add sugar; beat till fluffy. Add egg yolk and evaporated milk; beat well. (Mixture will look curdled.) Add flour mixture alternately with ⅓ cup *water* and beat well. Stir in coconut. Spoon about *3 tablespoons* batter into each paper bake cup-lined muffin cup. Bake in 350° oven 20 minutes or till lightly browned. Makes 20.

Lolita Pingol
Guiguinto, Philippines

Lumpia is a refreshing hot-weather meal. Shrimp, ham, pork, and vegetables make a flavorful filling for egg roll skins.

Index